Professor Shaul Sukenik

THE DEAD SEA

The world's ultimate natural healing resort for diseases of the
skin, joints, lungs and heart, among others

GW00598874

Professor Shaul Sukenik

The Dead Sea

The World's Ultimate Natural Healing Resort for Diseases
of the Skin, Joints, Lungs and Heart, Among Others

THE HEBREW UNIVERSITY MAGNES PRESS, JERUSALEM

Edited By Joan Hooper
Original Hebrew edition edited by Dafna Bar-On

ISBN 978-965-493-354-4

Printed in Israel
Typesetting: Ganit Rivin

This book is dedicated to the memory of my parents, who first met at the end of the 1930's at the Dead Sea, where my father, Dr. Shmuel Sukenik, worked as a doctor and my mother, Rachel Sukenik (née Singalovsky), worked as a nurse.

Table of Contents

Preface

The need for complementary and alternative medicine as a supplement to conventional medicine has grown steadily in recent years, as part of the attempt to find solutions that conventional medicine is unable to provide.

There is a significant difference between complementary medicine and alternative medicine. Complementary medicine, as the name implies, is offered in addition to conventional medicine, while alternative medicine is offered in its stead. We still lack conclusive scientific proof on the efficacy of most of the treatments offered by complementary and alternative medicine. More than a hundred different types of complementary and alternative medicine treatments are available, including acupuncture, medicinal herbs, food supplements, homeopathic medicine, massage therapy, naturopathic medicine, osteopathic medicine, the application of magnetic fields, chiropractics, and others. The number of people in Israel seeking complementary or alternative therapy is steadily increasing, just as it is throughout the western world. One study conducted in Israel showed an increase between 1993 and 2000 from 6% to 10% of all patients. Most of those seeking treatment have chronic skin or joint diseases, or malignant diseases.

Therapeutic Sites and Complementary/Alternative Medicine Sites

Many different kinds of complementary and/or alternative medicine treatments are offered at special therapeutic sites established in many countries, especially in Asia and Europe. While thousands of such therapeutic sites offer care to millions of patients every year, the efficacy of the treatments offered at these sites has not been tested or proven scientifically in prospective, controlled clinical studies. These therapeutic sites are established near natural springs or other sources of water believed to have therapeutic properties, next to fields of mud whose effectiveness has been proven in the treatment of joint diseases and other illnesses, or in areas where special climatic conditions prevail that assist in healing diseases, or at least in alleviating symptoms. For the most part, these therapeutic sites, which are located in isolated regions, far from large cities, so that the patients may benefit from a feeling that they are on vacation away from their daily concerns, have been shown to strengthen the immune system and reduce symptoms. Thus, a hotel situated in the center of a city or in a busy neighborhood that calls itself a hotel-spa cannot be considered a serious therapeutic site.

In Israel, the main and best known therapeutic site stretches along the western shore of the Dead Sea. In contrast to most other therapeutic sites around the world, this area has been chosen for many research studies conducted by researchers from Israel and abroad over the past forty years. These studies have proven the efficacy of the various types of treatment offered at the site as complementary therapy for a wide range of skin, rheumatic, heart and lung diseases, and many others. Some of these studies were encouraged and financed, in part or in their entirety, by the "Dead Sea R&D Tamar Regional Council D.N. Dead Sea", the Ministry of Tourism, the Ministry of Health, the national lottery (Mifal

Hapais) and many other institutions. The Israel Hotel Association has also made a significant contribution by providing free stays for patients participating in the studies. Despite the results of these studies, Israel has not yet decided to recognize this region as a national health resort. As a result, its acceptance into the International Society of Medical Hydrology and Climatology (ISMH) of countries with therapeutic sites based on unique natural treasures recognized by their governments has been delayed.

This book was written to provide the reader with basic information on spa medicine in general and on the Dead Sea region in particular. It describes the different types of diseases and the broad spectrum of treatments with proven efficacy, including regular drug treatment and treatments unique to the Dead Sea, their mechanism of action, their effect, their adverse effects and the pros and cons of sending patients to the Dead Sea region.

From the earliest days, mysterious healing properties have been attributed to water, which has been considered effective in the treatment of a wide range of diseases and pains. This belief is prominent among three of the world's great religions, Christianity, Islam and Judaism, as well as among many other religious communities around the world. The Bible relates the story of Naaman, a general in the army of the King of Aram, who, while a hero, suffered from leprosy. Because he was a great military figure, it seems reasonable to assume that the disease from which he suffered was not in fact leprosy, but rather psoriasis. The prophet Elisha recommended to Naaman that he bathe seven times in the water of the Jordan River. The bathing cured Naaman and turned his skin into that of a "young boy" (II Kings 5:1-14). It is well known that the ancient Egyptians used water for healing as far back as 4,000 years ago. Ruins of the oldest spa can be seen to this day in the city of Murano, Italy, where spring water was used for therapeutic purposes 5,000 years ago.

CHAPTER 1

A Historical Review of Water Therapy

Ancient Greece and the Roman Empire

The Greeks bathed in spring water and in seawater. Bathing in hot springs was the privilege of the wealthy alone, but hot baths were built later for the use of the common people. The legendary Greek poet Homer, who lived in the 9th century BCE, recommended the use of water for the treatment of fatigue, battle injuries to the heels and post-combat depression. Hippocrates (460-370 BCE), considered the father of modern medicine, recommended water therapy for joint pains, jaundice and paralysis. Hippocrates believed that all diseases are caused by a lack of balance in the body's fluids. He believed that therapy should include lifestyle changes, periodic bathing in spring water, excessive sweating (to remove pathogenic water from the body) and body massage.

Doctors of the Roman Empire period followed the lead of the Greeks and also recommended water therapy for arthritis, paralysis, urinary tract disease, battle wounds and problems related to athletes' musculoskeletal systems. They were the first to distinguish between treatment with hot water and cold water for different types of diseases or injuries. One of the famous physicians of that age, Asclepiades (124-40 BCE), who lived in Rome, established the foundations of hydrotherapy (treatment through bathing) and other treatments based on drinking water.

Rome had three types of baths: household, private and public. The public baths were especially spacious, allowing thousands of people to bathe at the same time. According to one study, every resident of Rome used an average of 1,400 liters of water every day, especially for bathing. We know that the amount of water consumed is considered, among others, an accepted index for living standard. It should be noted that in undeveloped countries of our own time, in homes without running water where water drawn from wells is used only for drinking, cooking and bathing, the average daily consumption is 50 liters per person. In developed countries, where running water is the standard and is used also for gardening, dishwashing, washing cars, etc., the average daily consumption is 400-500 liters per person. In Israel, the average daily consumption of water is about 300 liters per person.

The remains of luxurious baths built by the Romans can be found to this day in most of the countries of the Roman Empire, including Israel (at Massada for example). Some of these baths have been preserved down to the present time and are still used for therapy, for example, the baths in the English city, Bath.

The Middle Ages

After the fall of the Roman Empire, the use of baths declined, mostly because of opposition by the Catholic Church, which considered belief in the healing properties to water to be a form of idol worship and forbade its use for therapeutic purposes. Because they feared punishment by the Church, some of the residents avoided bathing in water for long periods of time. Some of the baths were used for new purposes, including conversion to houses of prayer. Only a few continued to function as bathing facilities, especially for use by the wealthy who didn't bow to the dictates of the Church.

From the 13th century on, water for therapeutic purposes slowly regained popularity, especially in Eastern Europe.

The Renaissance

The 16th century once again saw a certain decline in the popularity of public baths, some of which were closed because of the prevailing conviction that water brought with it diseases such as syphilis, plague and leprosy. And yet, many physicians in Italy recommended treatment at healing spas as a cure for disease. This period saw the beginning of experiments at defining the properties of water according to its chemical structure and mineral content. In 1594, the Italian doctor Minardo published a medical book listing 78 different diseases that could be treated successfully with water and mud. Two weeks of treatment with water, recommended by this physician, is the minimum period of treatment accepted to this day. In the wake of the popularity gained by these treatments various other countries followed in Italy's footsteps, especially France and Germany, which also began to develop this area of treatment.

At the beginning of the 17th century, the German doctor Sigmund Hahn began to use water in the treatment of diseases of the limbs, itching and other illnesses. It was during this period that treatment of these diseases was given the name used to this day, hydrotherapy – "treatment with water." In 1747, a book called "The easy way to treat most diseases" was published. Its author maintained that the use of water, whether by bathing at different temperatures, or drinking, leads to remedy or at least alleviation of symptoms for various diseases. Precise data concerning the efficacy of this form of therapy for chronic lead poisoning were gathered as early as 1767 at the famous English site in the city of Bath. The cause of the disease was the wide use of materials and products that contained large quantities of lead, now forbidden by every standard, in cosmetics, building materials, food coloring, wines and medicinal salts. The chronic poisoning was manifested by severe abdominal pain and various disturbances of the neurological system. According to the data, 95% of 281 patients who suffered from the disease and were treated by drinking or bathing in mineral water at the therapeutic site, either recovered entirely or experienced significant improvement. It is assumed that this impressive result was due to the greatly increased diuresis, which is characteristic of bathing in this water, and that the level of lead in the blood declined thanks to the increased secretion of this metal in the urine.

Modern Times

At the beginning of the 19th century, experiments were resumed in an attempt to determine the exact composition of spring water. Some doctors were convinced that every disease could be cured by bathing in the water of a specific spring, whose particular composition was best suited to the treatment and cure of that disease. In this period, doctors began to recommend combined treatments of bathing in hot and cold water, mud plasters, therapeutic plants, appropriate diet, physical activity, and body massage. Luxury hotels sprang up near the therapeutic springs, including the famous therapeutic spa in Baden-Baden, Germany. Baden-Baden quickly became a meeting place for the intellectual elite – public figures, artists, and politicians. Despite the flourishing of therapeutic spas in most European countries, in England, for example, most of the therapeutic spas were actually closed during this period. The well-known economic depression of the 1930s delivered a crippling blow to the spas.

After World War II, the spas once again flourished and became more accessible and appealing to the general public. In many countries, and especially those of the former communist bloc, these treatments were accepted in every way and their governments almost completely subsidized their development.

With the extensive development and popularity of alternative and complementary medicine hydrotherapy became more widely accepted and commonplace, but its high cost delayed any widespread increase in its use. The therapy itself is not expensive, rather it is the need to stay at hotels that adds to the cost and prevents the health care services in most countries from including it in official health care baskets. To persuade both the private and governmental insurers it is necessary to prove the efficacy of the treatments as well as their economic feasibility. For example, in recent years studies have started to appear showing that treatment at therapeutic sites for patients suffering from the inflammatory joint disease known as ankylosing spondylitis is less expensive than treatment provided by the combination of hospital stay and physical therapy.

Another factor that is holding back the development of this branch of medicine is the relative paucity of good, convincing prospective medical studies related to the efficacy of these treatments. Israeli investigators are now among the world's leaders in this field.

CHAPTER 2

Treatment at Health Resorts: Terms and Definitions

The therapeutic sites offer a wide variety of water treatments, which are explained in detail in this chapter.

Hydrotherapy

Hydrotherapy is a means of treatment based on bathing in fresh water with variable temperature that can be adjusted according to medical requirements. Hydrotherapy is conducted in both regular and therapeutic pools furnished with special devices intended for use in treating difficult cases, or designed for patients with severe physical limitations who cannot be treated without them. The treatment may involve total immersion of the body in water or immersion of only those parts of the body requiring specific treatment. The treatment is normally provided by a physical therapist specially trained for this kind of work. During treatment, the therapist enters the bath together with the patient or directs the patient from a position alongside the pool. The treatment also employs a variety of exercises (physical therapy) that are practiced while the patient is immersed in the pool.

Balneotherapy – Treatment With Mineral Water

By definition, mineral water contains at least one gram of solid material dissolved in one liter of water. The dissolved solid is usually salt (mineral) of some sort. There are different kinds of mineral water that differ from one another in the type and concentration of salts that they contain, giving them unique physical and chemical properties. At least nine different types of mineral water have been specified, according to the element or salt they contain in the greatest quantity. For example, sulfur water, which contains a significant quantity of sulfur, iron water, which contains a high concentration of iron compounds, calcium water, which contains a high concentration of calcium, alkaline water, which has an alkaline reaction, etc. We still cannot determine the ideal composition of mineral water or the best concentration of the various components required for optimal therapeutic use for a given disease. Each therapeutic site has a unique type of mineral water and only a few studies have compared the results of treatment provided to patients with a given disease, who have been treated with mineral water at two different therapeutic sites that differ one from the other in the type or concentration of mineral water found in them. The amount of minerals dissolved in the water of the Dead Sea or its springs is far greater than one gram of dissolved mineral content in one liter of water (approximately 340 grams) and its level of concentration is actually among the highest in the world.

Therapy based on the application of mineral water is called balneotherapy. The source of mineral water can be a deep underground spring, a lake, the sea or the open ocean. The heat of the water is not constant and a distinction is made between hypothermal water, whose temperature ranges from 20° to 32°C, thermal water, whose temperature ranges from 32° to 40°C, and hyperthermal water, whose temperature is over 40°C.

Spa Therapy

Spa therapy includes all of the treatments offered at therapeutic sites. The term "spa" has several possible definitions: in the Walloonian dialect of Belgium it is "espa," meaning a spring. To this day there is a small village in Belgium called Spa, near which a natural spring was discovered in the 14th century that was believed to be effective in the treatment of joint disease. According to another accepted definition, the term spa is a short rendition of the Latin words sanus per aquam – health through the use of water. Another possibility is a version of the Latin word spagere, meaning to disperse or spray water.

Mud Therapy – Pelotherapy

Most therapeutic sites also offer treatment based on applying mud over the entire body or parts of it (mud packs). The mud is generally heated to a temperature higher than that of mineral water – up to 40°C (129.6°F), or even higher. The mud is a mixture of non-organic materials (various minerals) and organic materials, which are usually the remains of plants, animals, or seaweed. Mud gathered for medical use is mined and sterilized to prevent infection when it is spread over the body, especially when used by people suffering from sores or other skin lesions. It also has to be rinsed clean of different substances such as small pebbles that may be hotter than the rest of the mud and cause burns. There are three main types of mud used for medical treatment: mud, moor, and peat, which are classified according to the quantities of their organic contents. The most common type is mud which is also used in the Dead Sea area. At some health sites the mud is dissolved in a tub of mineral water so that the two types of therapy are combined. This combined therapy is called peloma. Many health sites throughout the world, where mud is not found in the natural environment, import it from great distances. Today, mud can also be imported for household use and can be heated in a regular or microwave oven.

Climatotherapy

These treatments are based on climatic conditions unique to each site. We will describe climatotherapy in greater detail in the chapter on the Dead Sea health site.

Heliotherapy – Exposure to Solar Radiation

These treatments are based on exposure of the body to the sun's rays, including ultraviolet rays. This treatment will also be described in greater detail in the chapter on the Dead Sea health site.

Thalassotherapy

The word "thalasso" means sea or ocean water, and thalassotherapy is treatment based on bathing in sea or ocean water. Both of these contain a variety of minerals at varying concentrations that depends, for example, on the degree of heat and distance from the shore. Studies have shown that bathing in this water can result in an improvement in the condition of patients suffering from a variety of diseases.

Grottotherapy

Treatment offered in caves with unique climatic conditions, such as irradiation with radon gas, has been effective in the treatment of a number of joint diseases. A daily visit of several hours to a cave where random gas is emitted – in a concentration, of course, that does not constitute a health hazard and does not cause cancer – has proven effective in the treatment of patients suffering from a variety of inflammatory joint diseases, especially rheumatoid arthritis. This kind of therapy is not available in Israel.

CHAPTER 3

The Effect of Bathing on Physiological Systems

Bathing in both mineral and fresh water has a significant effect on the body's physiological systems. In this chapter the most important of these effects are described.

The Heart, Blood Vessels, and Kidneys

Immersion of the entire body, with the exception of the head, in either regular or mineral water, results in a large shifting of blood (about 700 ml) from the lower limbs and the abdominal cavity to the thorax and from there to the heart, due to an increase in hydrostatic pressure. The consequence of this flow is a significant increase in the amount of blood pumped by the heart (cardiac output) by as much as 30%, which persists as long as the patient remains in the water. This enhanced cardiac output also increases urine production with sodium and potassium excretion providing relief for patients suffering from diseases such as congestive heart failure, chronic liver disease, edema (swelling of the lower limbs), etc. In fact, any disease characterized by the accumulation of fluids can be alleviated by immersion of the body in water. Immersion also reduces the secretion of hormones such as renin and aldosterone. This also plays a beneficial role by increasing the secretion of salt in the urine. On the other hand, immersion reduces the secretion of anti-diuretic hormone whose function is to decrease the quantity of urine produced by the body. As a result, the suppression of this secretion, by immersion in water, also results in increased urine production. In general, bathing does not have any significant effect on systolic blood pressure (the high value) or diastolic blood pressure (the low value).

The Respiratory System

Oxygen consumption does not normally change when the body is at rest in water. It increases only when water temperature drops below 28°C (82.4°F), because of muscles tremors caused by the low temperature. Despite the increased quantity of blood in the chest cavity, which reduces lung expansion, there is no evidence that physical activity during immersion raises the maximum consumption of oxygen.

The Endocrine System (Glands of Internal Secretion)

Immersion increases secretion of the hormone known as cortisone. This hormone is produced and secreted by the adrenal glands that are situated next to the kidneys. Cortisone is one of the essential hormones, without which we cannot live. This hormone has many physiological roles, which we will not go into here. Cortisone is the most effective hormone for suppression of inflammatory processes, so that increasing its secretion by the adrenal glands significantly improves the condition of patients suffering from a wide range of inflammatory diseases, including arthritis. It has been proven that bathing in mineral water significantly increases blood levels of cortisone. Studies conducted in Jordan in 1990 showed that the secretion of hormones such as insulin and growth hormone is much greater in residents of the Dead Sea region than it is in residents of Amman, situated at an altitude of 766 meters (2,513 ft) above sea level. Thus, not only bathing in Dead Sea waters and its hot springs affects hormone secretion, but also the unique climatic conditions in the area. Increased secretion of insulin may improve the condition of some diabetics or delay the appearance of diabetes among residents of the area. Of course, for now, this remains an assumption only, which requires proof by prospective studies.

The increased activity of the peripheral nervous system (known as the sympathetic nervous system) seen during physical activity in patients immersed in water is lower than that seen during physical activity on land. The increase in heart rate recorded during activity when the body is immersed in water, which directly reflects sympathetic system activity, is more moderate because of the reduced secretion of the hormones epinephrine (adrenaline) and nor-epinephrine (nor-adrenaline) that increase the heart rate.

Muscle Activity

During physical activity, the muscles undergo anaerobic activity, in contrast with the aerobic activity that prevails at rest. For the muscles to function properly during physical effort the body must supply them with the energy required for their activity by means of metabolic cycles. The production of energy in these cycles leads to the accumulation of lactic acid in the blood. During physical activity in water the increase in lactic acid in the blood is more moderate than with the same physical activity out of water, a fact that suggests that muscle activity is easier and more efficient during immersion in water. This fact is important in the treatment of muscle injuries, in rehabilitation following sports injuries, in the treatment of patients with arthritis or patients suffering from muscular degeneration caused by insufficient activity.

Endorphins

The endorphins are produced and secreted by brain tissue and apparently by other tissues as well. There are several kinds of endorphins, which differ from each other in their structure and function. The structure of endorphins is similar to that of morphine so they are considered highly effective pain relievers. Increased secretion during bathing significantly relieves the suffering and pain of patients.

CHAPTER 4

The Dead Sea as a Health Resort

The Dead Sea is part of the Syro-African rift that stretches from the Taurus Mountains of Turkey to the Zimbazi Valley in South Africa, a distance of 6,000 kilometers. The Dead Sea is about 67 kilometers (41 miles) long and 18 kilometers (11 miles) at its maximum width and is the lowest spot on earth – 418 meters (1,371 ft) below sea level at its lowest point. The Dead Sea currently defines the border between Israel and the Kingdom of Jordan. The shores of the Dead Sea border the Judean Mountains on the west and the mountains of Edom on the east. According to geological theories, the sea was formed about two million years ago by the upheaval of earth between the Mediterranean Sea and the Syro-African Rift that caused a retreat of the Mediterranean waters that up to then covered the entire region.

The Dead Sea is divided into two parts, or basins: the northern basin, which is the larger and deeper of the two with a maximum depth of 400 meters (1,312 ft), and the southern basin, which is much smaller and very shallow – only a few meters in depth. In the past, the two basins were separated by a tongue of sea called Al-Lisan ("tongue" in Arabic). Today the two parts are separated by a narrow channel, which was dug to prevent the southern basin (which contains the Dead Sea evaporation pools) from drying out and disappearing.

The Dead Sea, which has no outlet, gets most of its water

from the Jordan River as well as from small streams that bring it relatively small amounts of sweet water. In the winter season it also receives a certain amount of precipitation that runs off the surrounding mountains.

The hot climate that prevails in the region causes evaporation of large quantities of water from the Dead Sea. In addition, diversion of water from the Jordan River by both Israel and Jordan for irrigation and drinking water has resulted in the "shrinking" of the Dead Sea. For example, in the past thirty years, the level of the Dead Sea has dropped by over 25 meters (82 ft) at a rate of 0.8 meters (2.62 ft) a year. Because the amount of water entering the Dead Sea is smaller than that evaporating from it, some see a danger that in the not very distant future it will dry out and disappear. Other scientists believe that the Dead Sea will not dry out entirely, since when the water level drops by another 100 meters (328 ft), a new balance will be established between the sources of water in the region, which will prevent its disappearance.

In the course of time, changes in the formation of the earth created underground streams. Large underground burrows remained in places where small rivers that once flowed into the Dead Sea ceased to exist. These burrows can collapse suddenly, without warning, creating deep pits known as sink holes that endanger the lives of residents and tourists in the region.

Minerals of the Dead Sea and Regional Springs

The Dead Sea is saltier than all other lakes, seas and oceans in the world, meaning that it contains a greater amount of dissolved salts than any other body of water on the earth. The amount of dissolved salt per liter ranges from 31.5 to 34.0 grams, an amount that is approximately ten times greater than that of the Mediterranean Sea (see Table 1). The waters are especially rich in magnesium, phosphates, sodium, chlorine and bromides (bromine compounds) and many other trace elements. In contrast, regular seawater contains cooking salt (mostly NaCl, which constitutes 95% of its salt), while Dead Sea water contains only 12%-15% sodium of its total mineral content. The salinity of Dead Sea water is even greater than that of the Great Salt Lake in the state of Utah, USA. The high concentration of salts, which gives the water a high specific gravity, enables people to float on the water's surface without fear of drowning. At the same time, swallowing a small amount of Dead Sea water may cause complications, a phenomenon that will be discussed in the chapter on adverse effects of balneotherapy.

Nuns living in the area named the sea the "Dead Sea," because they believed that because of its high degree of salinity no creature could live in it. This assumption has proved to be mistaken. In 1936, a young Israeli researcher named Eliezer Volcani published an article in one of the world's most prestigious scientific journals that contained the results of his study, according to which a number of unicellular creatures (bacteria) have developed unique mechanisms allowing them to live in the Dead Sea. In recognition of his discovery, one of the bacteria discovered in the Dead Sea was named after him – *Halopherax volcan*. Several years ago, Ukrainian researchers found that besides the unicellular bacteria discovered by the Israeli scientist at least three types of fungi live in the Dead Sea. It is interesting to note that researchers have been successful in breeding these fungi in regular laboratory cultures only when water containing a 50% concentration of Dead Sea water is added to the substrate. That is, not only do the fungi grow in salt water, but they need the high salt concentration to continue developing.

Mineral water emanates from more than a dozen underground springs near the Dead Sea. The temperature of the water in these springs ranges from 28° to 30°C (82.4° to 86.0°F). The most famous of these springs are called Hamei Zohar, Hamei Mazor, Hamei Shalem, Maayonot Ein Gedi, Hamei Yesha, Hamei Ein Tamar, Hamei Ein Hakikar and Hamei Ein No'it. They are sometimes referred to as sulfur springs, because they contain different compounds of sulfur that give them an unpleasant smell similar to that of rotten eggs. But the name is not justified, because it is not yet known precisely which components have the most beneficial effect on patients' symptoms. The amount of minerals dissolved in the waters of these springs is much less than that of the Dead Sea, but still much more than that of all other health springs in the world (see Table 2).

Trace Elements

In addition to its primary minerals, the waters of the Dead Sea and the hot springs also contain miniscule quantities of many other substances known as trace elements. They are of great importance because a deficiency of one or more of these substances can affect the proper functioning of the immune system. For example, we know that patients suffering from rheumatoid arthritis often have a deficiency in zinc and some researchers have reported that the oral administration of zinc results in a degree of improvement in the condition of some patients. Another example is a surplus of copper, also considered a trace element, which may cause deterioration in the condition of patients suffering from rheumatoid arthritis, so that drugs that reduce blood copper levels can improve their condition. As mentioned above, trace elements are found in different concentrations in Dead Sea water and in the water of the surrounding springs (see Table 3).

Medicinal Mud

Medicinal mud used for therapy at the Dead Sea health resort is mined at specific sites along the shore of the sea. For the most part, it is black in color and is called "black mud." This mud contains two principal components: organic and inorganic. The inorganic components are the various salts in the mud that are related to its various earth components. The organic component contains the remains of living organisms, seaweed and various plants. In the Dead Sea region only the kind of material known as "mud" is used. This kind of mud is comprised mostly of inorganic materials – high concentrations of various salts and minerals, including important trace elements (see Table 4).

One of the characteristics of the mud used at the Dead Sea is its ability to preserve its heat for a long time after it has been applied to the body – its temperature decreases at a rate of one degree centigrade every ten minutes. In addition to this effect – beneficial in itself – of the heat on surrounding joints and tissues such as tendons, ligaments and muscles, the mud increases the secretion of different chemical compounds that suppress the inflammatory process, and reduces or blocks the secretion of other compounds that accelerate it. The mud also increases the secretion of antioxidants whose function is to protect the various tissues from the free oxygen radicals produced in metabolic processes that tend to cause oxygenation, wich can cause tissue damage. The role of the antioxidants, including vitamin C, vitamin A, vitamin E, selenium, and others, is to prevent the oxygenation of these radicals. Studies conducted, especially in Italy, have shown that mud packs can increase the secretion of antioxidants and thereby improve the condition of patients suffering from arthritis, a disease sometimes characterized by increased secretion of free radicals. It is worth noting that recent studies have shown that Dead Sea mud also has properties that inhibit the development of various bacteria. The addition of Dead Sea mud to bacterial cultures such as E. Coli, Staphylococcus aureus and others suppresses their growth.

Table 1. The composition of Dead Sea water in comparison to Mediterranean Sea and ocean water. The values are in milligrams per liter.

Element	Dead Sea	Mediterranean	Ocean
Chloride	224,900	22,900	19,000
Magnesium	44,000	1,490	1,350
Sodium	40,100	12,700	10,500
Calcium	17,200	470	400
Potassium	7,650	476	390
Bromide	5,300	76	65

Table 2. Water composition of a mineral spring (Hamei Zohar). The values are in milligrams per liter.

Element	Composition
Chloride	35,509.5
Bromide	769.5
Bicarbonate	185.5
Sulphate	677.5
Lithium	3.66
Sodium	8,595.0
Potassium	825.0
Calcium	3,600.0
Magnesium	5,830.0
Stronthium	52.5

Table 3. Trace elements in the water of the Ein Gedi spring. The values are in micrograms per liter.

Element	Concentration
Arsenic (As)	1.0
Cadmium (Cd)	0.1
Chrome (Cr)	10.0
Copper (Cu)	59.0
Mercury (Hg)	0.1
Selenium (Sc)	1.0
Lead (Pb)	11.0
Zinc (zn)	45.0
Cobalt (Co)	23.0
Nickel (Ni)	27.0
Molibdenum (mo)	10.0
Vanadium (va)100.0	100.0
Silver (Ag)	1.0

Table 4: The main elements of Dead Sea mud. The values are in milligrams per liter.

Element	Concentration
Mg	32,503
Na	31,734
Ca	23,547
K	6,835
Cl	190,000
Total Salinity	2,784,625

The Medical History of the Dead Sea

The Dead Sea is referred to by many names. It is also called the

East Sea, the Arava Sea, Lot's Sea, the Zohar Sea, the Sodom Sea, the Gomorrah Sea and the Salt Sea, among others. The Greeks called it the "Asphalt Sea" because of the material that looked like asphalt that was drawn from its waters and served many purposes, medicinal and non-medicinal. It is assumed that the biblical cities of Sodom and Gomorrah were situated on the south coast of the sea. The nearby city of Jericho is considered to be the oldest city in the world (Kings II, Chapter 2, verses 19-23). We read of the prophet Elisha who added salt to the water of a spring near Jericho to purify it, thereby ending the epidemic which killed many residents of the area who used this water for drinking and to irrigate their fields and water their flocks of sheep.

The Egyptian Queen Cleopatra, who lived in the first century BCE and was thought to be one of the most beautiful women of her time, was known for her great love of beauty and health products. She believed that the waters of the Dead Sea contained substances that were beneficial to health and established industries in the area for the production of perfumes and beauty care products. Various compounds, essences and ointments were produced or compounded from the waters of the Dead Sea together with plants that grew along its shores and in the area of Jericho. Of these, the most important was the balsam tree, a member of the pine family, whose branches, trunk, leaves and seeds were used to make products for beauty care and an ointment to treat sores. In Europe, where widespread use was made of the ointment, it was called Jerusalem Balsam. Medicines derived from this tree also were used in the treatment of headaches and visual impairments of various types, including impaired vision due to cataracts. Material produced from this tree was also used to improve the taste of wine. Local residents, who earned their living in this endeavor, kept the secret of the processes used for production of the medicine and perfume made from the balsam tree.

The Nabateans living in the region used to sell the Egyptians a black material known as bitumen (similar to black tar) that they extracted from the seawaters. The Egyptians used bitumen for body stuffing and mummification. The bitumen was also used for calking and sealing boats and was called Jews' tar. It was also used as a medicinal substance to prevent muscular spasms (of the abdominal muscles, for example), to heal wounds, to mend broken bones and stop bleeding from skin wounds. Gladiators who fought in the arena frequently used bitumen ointment to stop bleeding and hasten the healing of their wounds, and Muslim doctors used it as a medicine for the treatment of infections caused by worms. King Herod, who built the famous winter palace at Massada, also built therapeutic and pleasure pools for the use of the soldiers of the Roman legions. Josephus Flavius mentions the waters of these hot springs and notes that it is even possible to drink the water for therapeutic purposes. When Herod became ill, his doctors recommended bathing in the spring waters, a treatment that in the end didn't prevent his death, apparently from end stage kidney failure. The rich residents of Rome used to import by sea large containers of Dead Sea water for bathing at home in luxurious baths. As is well known, ancient scrolls of great scientific and historical value were discovered in the Dead Sea region, but to our great surprise, there is almost no reference in them to the therapeutic properties of the region.

In the Byzantine period, several monasteries were built in the area and many Crusaders made pilgrimage to them. Bedouin tribes have also lived in the area for hundreds of years, but we have no information about use made by the Bedouin or the Crusaders of the therapeutic products of the Dead Sea, or of their bathing in its waters for therapeutic purposes.

In 1772, the French scientist Lavoisier (whom most of us remember from our chemistry lessons at school) published the first analysis of the composition of Dead Sea water, and in 1889 the famous French scientist, Joseph Louis Gay-Lussac, published a further analysis of its composition.

The visionary founder of the Jewish State, Benjamin Ze'ev Herzl, mentioned, in his speeches as far back as 1902, that the waters of the Dead Sea are rich in bromine, sulfur and phosphates that can be produced, used and even traded commercially. In 1911, the Russian Jewish mining engineer, Moshe Novomeysky, who later immigrated to Israel, visited the country and was highly impressed by the enormous commercial potential in the production of different minerals from the Dead Sea. In 1920, he applied to the British Mandate authorities for a franchise to produce these minerals. In 1930, Israel Potash Industry, Ltd., was established and in 1932 it began the production of potash.

The first plant to be built was situated in the northern area of the sea, around Kalia. Jews and Arabs worked together in the plant and produced potassium and potassium salts. My father, blessed is his memory, Dr. Shmuel Sukenik, to whose memory this book is dedicated, worked for two years in this plant as its only doctor, treating both Jewish and Arab workers with dedication. A second plant was built later, in 1934, in the southern region, near Sodom, and this is the plant now known as the Dead Sea Industries, which is the fourth largest plant in the world for production of potash. Other important materials, required by various industries, are produced from the waters of the Dead Sea including magnesium chloride, aluminum chloride, industrial salts, antifreeze, cooking salt and raw materials for the cosmetics industry.

Following the creation of the State of Israel, scientists and physicians from all over the world began to show interest in the unique healing properties of Dead Sea water and since then have written and published hundreds of studies proving the importance of the region as a unique therapeutic site.

The Unique Climatic Conditions at the Dead Sea

According to the well-known author, Mark Twain, "Everybody complains about the weather, but nobody does anything about it." The weather in the Dead Sea region is far from being pleasant for those who live there, but it has unique qualities that alleviate the suffering of patients with a wide variety of illnesses, including joint disease, skin disease, heart disease and lung disease, among others. In this chapter we will describe and explain the unique climatic conditions of the region and the effect they have on various illnesses.

Ultraviolet Rays

Ultraviolet rays are invisible to the human eye. There are two kinds of ultraviolet rays, distinguished one from the other by their wavelength: UVA, whose wavelength is between 320 and 400 nanometers, and UVB, whose wavelength is between 280 and 320 nanometers. UVB rays, which cause sunburn, are more harmful to humans. As a result of the high temperatures characteristic of the region on most days of the year and the paucity of clouds that block the sun's rays, the Dead Sea region is characterized by evaporation of large quantities of water from the sea surface, which creates a vapor haze. This haze blocks the UVB rays (the harmful rays) more than it blocks UVA (the good rays). The fact that the Dead Sea is the lowest spot on earth – 400 meters (1,312 ft) or more below sea level – increases the distance traveled by the ultraviolet rays before they reach land, UVB more than UVA rays. The ratio between UVB and UVA, therefore, is the highest anywhere on the face of the earth. In fact, this difference in the nature of ultraviolet radiation between this region and all other regions makes it beneficial in the healing of several skin diseases, including psoriasis. The unique radiation in the region also reduces the risk of sunburn due to exposure to the sun and allows patients to remain in the sun for longer periods of time than they could do in other places.

Atmospheric and Barometric Pressure

Atmospheric pressure is the force exerted by the weight of air in the earth's atmosphere. Atmospheric pressure is measured in units called "atmospheres." One atmosphere is the pressure exerted by a column of air at sea level. Heat and cold affect the weight of air and thus the atmospheric pressure, but their effect is small and insignificant. The atmospheric pressure at the Dead Sea, which is the highest in the world, has a beneficial effect on a broad range of diseases, particularly on joint diseases, chronic lung diseases, heart diseases and others.

Atmospheric pressure is measured with a barometer, which is a tube filled with mercury, closed at its upper end and immersed in a bowl of mercury that is open to the air (similar to the instrument used for measuring blood pressure, which is also based on a column of mercury). The pressure of one atmosphere at sea level at 0°C (32°F) is equal to a mercury column 760 millimeters high. In fact, "barometric pressure" and "atmospheric pressure" are interchangeable terms. Atmospheric pressure, for example, decreases by 50% for every ascent of 5.5 kilometers (3.42 miles). The lower the point below sea level, the greater the barometric pressure, so that in the Dead Sea region it is the highest in the world – about 800 millimeters of mercury.

Studies conducted in the United States in the 1960s proved that an increase in barometric pressure usually results in alleviation of joint pains. When an American millionaire heard the report of studies conducted with his funding, he replied in surprise: "That's it? – you could have gotten all of that information about the effect of weather from my wife, without needing studies like these." And in fact it is well known that arthritis patients can occasionally serve as weather forecasters, predicting oncoming rain. The explanation for this is simple: before the onset of rain, there is a decrease in atmospheric pressure, called a barometric depression. This depression causes an increase or reappearance of pain, so that the patients know that rain is on the way.

Humidity and Relative Humidity

"Humidity" is the degree of moisture in the air. It can be measured in terms of absolute humidity or relative humidity: "Absolute humidity" is the mass of water found in a specific mass of air; "relative humidity" is the ratio, expressed in percentage, between the quantity of vapor (water) in the air (at a given volume and temperature) and the amount of vapor that the same volume of that air can contain when it is fully saturated. The maximum quantity of vapor the air can contain depends on its temperature. The higher the temperature, the greater the amount of water vapor it can hold, and the lower the temperature, the less it can hold. The explanation for this lies in the fact that relative humidity is derived from the balance between the rate of evaporation and the rate of condensation (the creation of water vapor) of the water molecules. The lower the temperature is the greater is the condensation relative to evaporation.

As a result, in addition to barometric pressure, humidity and temperature play a significant role through their effect on the symptoms of patients suffering from joint diseases. As long ago as 1948, Swedish investigators built special hospital rooms in which the temperature and humidity could be controlled. They housed patients suffering from various types of joint diseases in these rooms for approximately 100 days and proved that at high temperatures – about 32°C – (89.6°F) and relatively low humidity (about 35%), most of the patients experienced improvement in their condition. For the most part, relatively low humidity brings relief of joint pain. At the Dead Sea the humidity is relatively low: approximately 33% from April to September and 40-50% during the rest of the year. The uniform high temperature, which in the summer months ranges from 32°C to 40°C (89.6°F to 104°F) and during the winter months ranges between 20°C and 24°C (68°F to 75.2°F), also reduces joint pain.

The season of the year also affects symptoms. Sometimes we see worsening in a patient's condition during the winter months, which is almost certainly a result of the decreased barometric pressure and increased humidity. In the summer, on the other hand, most patients experience relief.

In studies conducted in Israel in the 1990s by Prof. Abraham Weinberger and his team, it was found that joint pains were affected by barometric pressure, temperature, and humidity. It was also found that women are more sensitive than men to changes in the weather. It is interesting to note that even after knee replacement surgery, in which the patient's knee is replaced by an artificial one, weather continues to affect pain symptoms in the implant. Various studies have shown that a paucity of precipitation is beneficial for joint pains so that this factor, which is also characteristic of the Dead Sea region, is of some importance.

Oxygen-enriched Air

As is well known, the saturation of oxygen in air decreases as we ascend to higher altitudes (above sea level). The opposite is also true: the lower we descend below sea level, the "richer" the air becomes in oxygen, in addition to barometric (atmospheric) pressure. Because of this difference in barometric pressure, the amount of oxygen inhaled into the lungs is significantly greater at the Dead Sea than anywhere else. The high level of oxygen contained by the air there has a beneficial effect on patients suffering from chronic lung and heart diseases.

Low Level of Allergens (Substances That Cause Allergies) in the Air

It has long been known that the number of people suffering from asthma increases in places rich in vegetation, where pollen from trees, plants and flowers is found in high concentrations in the air. The relatively small number of plants and trees in the Dead Sea region reduces the amount of allergens carried by wind that could result in an increased severity of asthma attacks, or even cause them. It should be noted that the small number of industries located in the region also reduces air pollution and the emission of toxic substances that have a harmful effect on asthma patients.

The concentration of bromine in the air

Because of the high level of evaporation of water from the Dead Sea that contains a high concentration of bromine salts, the amount of bromine in the air is approximately twenty times greater than in other places. When we inhale Dead Sea air over a period of several weeks, the amount of bromine in our blood also rises significantly. Not very long ago, bromine was used in the production of tranquilizers, and before the appearance of Valium most tranquilizers contained bromine salts. The soothing effects of bromine salts explains the feeling of peace and calm experienced by many people who stay in the Dead Sea region, so that we may consider bromine to be the region's quality version of Valium.

CHAPTER 5

Health Resorts for Rheumatic Diseases

Introduction

Rheumatic diseases are diseases of the joints. The joints are anatomic structures that join two bones. Hippocrates was the first to use the term "rheuma," meaning pains emanating from the joints. He believed that rheuma was a fluid produced by the brain that, when it leaked from the brain and descended to the body, was liable to cause inflammation in the joints that it infiltrated. Doctors who treat joint diseases are rheumatologists. In Israel rheumatology has been recognized as a separate field of specialization for the past 15 years. Only a specialist in internal medicine can specialize further in rheumatology. To become a specialist in rheumatology, the physician must pass examinations of the Israel Medical Association Scientific Council. It is important to note that orthopedics is a separate and distinct field and even though rheumatic diseases are sometimes also treated by orthopedic surgeons, in most cases it is preferable that a rheumatologist provide the treatment.

More than a hundred different types of rheumatic diseases are known. Most joint diseases are acquired diseases, while only a few are considered inherited diseases. These diseases can appear at any age, from childhood to old age. Some are found more commonly in women, others in men, while still others are found at equal rates among men and women alike. Similarly, some of the acquired diseases appear more frequently among patients with a particular genetic makeup and in these individuals the disease also may be more severe than in others. The disease may affect one joint – monoarthritis, a few joints (two to five joints) – oligoarthritis, or more than five joints – polyarthritis. The joint involvement may be symmetric or asymmetric and sometimes it changes from one form to another, or the number of joints affected may change. The causes of joint disease are unknown in most of its forms, so it is difficult to cure. In cases where the cause of the disease is known, such as when the inflammation in the joint is caused by penetration of a germ into the joint, the patient can be cured with antibiotics. These relatively rare cases are known as septic arthritis.

Joint diseases are divided into two primary categories: inflammatory and non-inflammatory. In contrast to a common public misconception, rheumatic diseases cannot be healed by antibiotics because the inflammation is usually sterile and not caused by germs. The most common inflammatory diseases (inflammatory arthritis) that can be treated successfully at the Dead Sea, among other places, are rheumatoid arthritis, psoriatic arthritis, ankylosing spondylitis, and others. The non-inflammatory diseases that can be treated successfully are, for example, osteoarthritis and fibromyalgia.

The Structure of the Joint

A joint is created by the connection of two bones to each other. The ends of the bones are composed of cartilage. The joint itself is hermetically sealed by the joint capsule, which is composed of rigid, connective tissue (Fig. 1). The inside of the capsule is coated with an especially delicate tissue, called synovia. This tissue covers the entire interior surface of the joint up to the cartilage. The cells of the synovial tissue produce a special fluid (synovial fluid), which is secreted into the joint space. One of the most important functions of this fluid is to facilitate the movement of the joint, in the way that motor oil reduces friction and improves the function of a car engine. Every normal joint has a small amount of this fluid. When inflammation develops in the joint an abnormally large quantity of the fluid is produced, giving the joint a swollen appearance.

Cartilage tissue is characterized by a relatively small number of cartilage cells, so that it is ineffective in renewing itself, when needed, in comparison with other kinds of tissues such as, for example, skin or liver tissue. As a result, cumulative damage to the cartilage will in time result in tissue "wear and tear". There are still no effective drugs available to accelerate the growth of cartilage or prevent its deterioration. There are products that contain various components of cartilage tissue, which advertisers claim can renew cartilage and hasten the repair of damage. The aggressive advertising in the electronic and print media of these products, which are only food additives and not drugs, is deceptive, based on insufficient facts and not yet proven by serious scientific studies. The tissue does not contain blood vessels that feed it directly, but is fed primarily by diffusion via the synovial fluid and through the bone tissue next to it. The cartilage also does not have nerve fibers, so that direct damage to it does not cause pain.

Other structures that are also susceptible to inflammation are found outside and close to the joint capsule. These structures, including muscles that attach to the bones close to the joint and bursas, which are spaces whose interior is also covered with synovial tissue and whose function is to facilitate muscular contraction, are frequently involved. The human body contains approximately 168 bursas, located for the most part next to the points where muscles attach to bones. These are extremely slippery parts that reduce the friction that accompanies muscle contractions and thus improve muscle function. Bursas are sometimes connected to the joint capsule. If fluid accumulates in the capsule it can also fill a bursa that under normal conditions contains only a very small amount of the fluid. For example, around the knee joint, like every large joint, there are several bursas. These are above and below the patella (kneecap), behind the knee, etc., so that in the case of an accumulation of "water" on the knee, swelling may take place behind the knee as a result of the flow of fluid from the real knee cavity into the bursa behind it, which is known as Baker's bursa.

In addition to the bursas and the muscles, tendons and ligaments are also located outside and close to the joint. As with joints, some of the tendons are also enclosed in a sheath, with synovial tissue located between the sheath and the tendon. For this reason, inflammation of the synovial tissue will cause swelling of the tendons as well as the injured joint.

The source of the pain, which is the primary symptom of inflamed joints, is uncertain. The pain fibers do not penetrate into the joint itself, but are located only inside the tissue of the capsule. Many pain fibers are located outside the joint space, in muscles fibers for example. Thus, neither the patient nor even the doctor can specify the source of the pain precisely, to determine if the problem is inside or outside the joint. Frequently, patients believe that the source of their pain is in the joint itself, while the real source is located outside the joint – in the muscle or tendon. It should be noted that this problem of inability to specify the exact source of the pain is not only characteristic of joint diseases but of all diseases involving internal organs or systems, because the representation of the nerve fibers, which conduct the pain, in the cerebral cortex is limited in comparison with the representation of the skin, for example. It is therefore easy to determine precisely the source of pain in a skin injury caused, for example, by a needle prick, even with closed eyes, yet it is quite impossible to determine the source of pain if it is in the heart, stomach, kidneys, etc. This is equally true if the pain originates, for example, in the hip joint. It can be felt through the entire length of the thigh or even in the backside, and a pain that originates in the shoulder can be felt elsewhere, in the arm, for example. This is similar to pain caused by a heart attack that can sometimes be felt only in the shoulder, neck or back. The phenomenon of a pain that is felt in a place far from its actual source is called "referred" pain.

Diagnosis of Arthritis

The most effective means of diagnosing arthritis is by physical examination. Laboratory tests and various imaging procedures such as x-ray, bone scan, ultrasound, CT or MRI are less important and cannot always confirm or rule out the diagnosis of arthritis. Sometimes, months, or even years can pass before a definitive diagnosis of arthritis can be made with one of these procedures. There are well-known cases in which, even though the arthritis was active and severe, the laboratory tests indicated an entirely normal condition. In other words, the clinical findings do not always correlate well with the results of imaging or laboratory tests. Physical examination enables the doctor to establish the presence or absence of signs of arthritis. These include pain when the joint is moved or palpated, the presence of swelling, local heat or erythema (redness), accumulation of fluid in the joint space, or limited range of movement in the affected joint. Usually, only some of these findings are detected during the examination.

Potential Mechanisms of Action for the Treatment of Arthritis With Water

The mechanisms that lead to relief following bathing in mineral water or the application of heated mud treatments have not yet been sufficiently clarified. Apparently, there are several mechanisms that operate simultaneously and complement each other, among which the most important are mechanical, thermal and chemical mechanisms.

Mechanical Mechanisms

Increased hydrostatic pressure and the buoyancy effect of mineral water, which increase as the specific gravity increases (as in the Dead Sea), make it possible to move the affected joints more easily and increase their range of movement. Improvement in range of joint movement is of great importance, since it helps to delay the development of permanent deformity and slows disease progress.

As mentioned, various studies have proved that it is possible to reduce soft tissue swelling around the affected joint and in the joint itself by increasing the amount of urine produced while bathing. Similarly, the reduction of pain felt while bathing increases patients' motivation to cooperate and attain a better range of joint movement.

Thermal Mechanisms

Heating the body by bathing in regular water or in mineral water, or by the application of mudpacks, is of great importance and works in different ways. Heat increases the secretion of hormones like cortisone that block inflammatory processes and of endorphins that suppress pain. The secretion of these hormones increases as the temperature of the water rises (above 34°C), or in the case of mineral water with a high concentration of salts compared to regular tap water. Heat also decreases the secretion of different proteins that enhance symptoms of inflammation such as the protein called rheumatoid factor. It has been proven that mud packs suppress the secretion of different pro-inflammatory substances. Heating the body also significantly affects the immune system, in particular cell types such as different lymphocytes, which are known to accelerate inflammation. Heat is one of the factors that delays the activity of these cells and even reduces their number. Frequently, heat has a beneficial affect on the injured tissues alongside the joint itself, such as tendons, ligaments and the joint capsule (the tissue that envelops the joint) and its warmth can improve the range of joint movement.

Chemical Effects

The chemical composition of mineral water and mud also includes many elements known as trace elements, among which are zinc, copper, iron, selenium, lithium, manganese, rubidium, etc. Some arthritis patients are deficient in one or more of these trace elements. It has been reported that in some cases the addition of oral zinc improves the condition of patients suffering from various types of arthritis. A debate is currently being conducted in the medical literature over the question of whether some of these trace elements are absorbed through the skin and from there into the blood vessels after bathing or the application of mud packs. The prevailing opinion among researchers is that there is no significant absorption of these elements through the skin and that their blood level does not rise, but it is possible that some of them are indeed absorbed into the skin only, as can be seen by the affect of the Dead Sea on the skin disease known as psoriasis. Because these substances have extremely low blood levels in any event, it is very hard to know if there is any degree of absorption.

Other Influences

Rest, per se, at a luxurious spa hotel, far from the pressures of earning a living or of family quarrels can have a beneficial effect on most joint diseases as well as on other illnesses. Studies have proven that rest and stress reduction have a beneficial affect on the immune system and on patients' symptoms, and are a significant part of the treatment plan. Thus, a hotel situated within a large city that defines itself as a spa hotel, in which treatments can be had without staying on site for several days or weeks, is less effective than a health resort that includes not only the spa but also other possible treatments, and especially a restful environment, stress reduction, a unique climate, etc.

Rheumatic Diseases

a) Rheumatoid Arthritis

Rheumatoid arthritis can appear at any age, but most cases occur in the third or fourth decade of life. The disease occurs in the adult population at a frequency of 1-2% and affects women more than men (up to three times as often), usually involves many joints, both large and small, and usually in a symmetrical pattern. The cause of the disease is unknown, but people with a specific genetic makeup are more liable to develop the disease, which in their case is sometimes more severe than in those who don't have that genetic makeup. Whatever causes the disease produces inflammation of the synovial tissue found in every joint. The inflammation changes this tissue, which is normally extremely delicate, into tissue that is similar in its biological behavior to tumor tissue. It grows quickly and uncontrolably, it penetrates into cartilage and bone and the inflammatory cells that it contains secrete various substances that increase the severity of the inflammation and cause irreversible damage to the joint. This damage can be seen on x-rays as erosion of the bone. These "erosions" can appear within less than a year of the first appearance of the disease and only infrequently can they be cured completely. Rheumatoid arthritis is a multi-system disease that can affect, in addition to the joints, tendons and bursas, which are also covered with synovial tissue, other systems such as the lungs, heart, eyes and blood vessels. The appearance of the disease is sometimes characterized by systemic symptoms such as low-grade fever, fatigue, weakness, lack of appetite, loss of weight, enlargement of the lymph glands and spleen, so that valuable time sometimes passes before a correct diagnosis is reached. Another characteristic of all rheumatic diseases is "morning stiffness" – the patient feels bad when he wakes up in the morning and this feeling is mainly characterized by a sense of stiffness and inability to move the inflamed joints. This feeling can continue for as long as several hours. The longer it persists the more severe the disease. Some patients feel a sensation of dryness in the mouth and eyes, which is also characteristic of other inflammatory diseases as well as other diseases of the immune system. Approximately one-third of all patients have small lumps under the skin, near the joints and especially around the elbows, whose size can reach as much as a few centimeters. These lumps are called rheumatoid nodules and they appear mainly among patients suffering from active, severe disease. It is very important to diagnose the disease as early as possible, before the first appearance of erosions. The earlier the disease is detected the greater the chance of successful therapy.

Most of the diagnostic parameters for the disease, accepted throughout the world, are clinical parameters, which are diagnosed by physical examination. Only a few are based on imaging or laboratory tests.

Most laboratory tests used for this disease are non-specific and only indicate the presence of an inflammatory process. Only one test, called the "rheumatoid factor" test, is more specific. This factor is a protein that appears in the blood of approximately one-third of patients, especially patients in whom the disease is active and severe. This test is also not sufficiently specific and can appear in other diseases as well.

Since the cause of the disease is unknown, it cannot be cured and many patients develop deformities in the joints over the years that cause great suffering and a significant reduction in their quality of life. The disease is also liable to result in a significant reduction of life expectancy. Some patients also suffer from heart disease caused by damage to the coronary arteries. Yet despite this, it is interesting to note that the disease is less common among smokers, although, of course, this is not a good enough reason to start smoking.

Drug Therapy

As mentioned above, diagnosis at the earliest possible stage is of great importance so that treatment can be started as early as possible, thus increasing the chances that the patient will respond to the treatment and enter remission before the development of erosions.

Patients suffer mostly from joint pain and everything possible should be done to alleviate this pain. In principle, the pain can be treated with any painkiller. A distinction is made among several different groups of painkillers. One group includes simple drugs that suppress mild to moderate pains but do not affect the inflammatory process. This group includes drugs such as paracetamol, propoxyphene, dipyrone, and many others. The second group includes anti-inflammatory drugs that do not contain steroids (hormones of the cortisone type), known as NSAIDs – non-steroidal anti-inflammatory drugs. This group includes many drugs that have been used widely for the past 40 years, some of which can now be purchased over the counter. It includes diclofenac, indomethacin, naproxen, ibuprofen, etodolac, piroxican, nimesalide, nabumetone, and many others. All of these drugs are effective in reducing pain and inflammation, but all have adverse effects that may sometimes be life threatening. The adverse effects are caused by injury to the upper and lower digestive tract. The drugs can cause severe heartburn, abdominal pain, and ulcers in the stomach or duodenum, which can lead to serious bleeding and/or perforation of the organ's wall. In contrast to common wisdom, taking drugs in the form of suppositories does not reduce the frequency of adverse effects. Other common adverse effects are skin rashes, elevated blood pressure and impaired liver and kidney function tests. These adverse effects sometimes appear after only a few days or weeks of treatment. The longer the drugs are used, the greater the risk and the complication rate. NSAIDs are prohibited for some patients, so patients are advised to consult with a doctor before taking them, and should be on the alert for the appearance of possible adverse effects. As stated above, these drugs can be dangerous and can even cause death. For example, in 1999 over 16,000 people died in the United States from digestive tract complications, similar to the number of deaths caused by AIDS that year. It is important to know and to stress that the drugs in this group cannot cure the disease or halt its progress, but only reduce the pain and inflammation.

Cox 2 Inhibitors

This is a third new group of painkillers and anti-inflammatory drugs. Because of the adverse effects of NSAIDs on the digestive tract, which make their use unsafe, this new group of drugs has been developed in recent years with similar efficacy for joint pain and inflammation, but much less significant effects on the digestive tract. The drug most of us remember from this group, which attained great success when it was introduced, is rofecoxib. Other drugs in this group are cebecoxib and etoricoxib. However, it quickly became apparent that these drugs are liable to cause a slight increase in blood pressure and in the frequency of heart attacks. These unexpected findings resulted in the voluntary withdrawal of rofecoxib from general use by the Merck pharmaceutical company, despite the great efficacy of the drug in relieving pain. Later, other drugs of this new group were withdrawn even before they were put on the market. In Israel two drugs of this group, cebecoxib and etoricoxib, are still in use, but they should be used wisely, in general, and their use for patients suffering from severe heart disease, including congestive heart failure, uncontrolled hypertension or impaired kidney function should be limited. Even with the administration of drugs from this group the progress of the disease cannot be halted.

Disease-Modifying Anti-Rheumatic Drugs

When the diagnosis of rheumatoid arthritis is certain the disease must also be treated with drugs belonging to a group called "disease-modifying anti-rheumatic drugs" (DMARD). The use of drugs in this group supplements the use of drugs in the NSAIDs group or COX 2 inhibitors, which only relieve pain and do not halt the progress of the disease. The most important and most effective of the drugs in this group include:

1. Gold salt injections

In the past, gold salt injections administered once a week were considered to be a highly effective drug, but in recent years more effective drugs have been developed and the use of gold injections has disappeared almost entirely. They also necessitate weekly blood and urine tests because they can cause damage to the bone marrow or the kidneys, adverse effects that can be detected at an early stage only by means of these tests.

2. Salazopyrine (Sulfasalazine)

A drug administered in daily doses in capsule form that is still in common use. This drug is also liable to cause injury to the digestive system as well as skin rashes, in addition to impairing liver function and blood counts, so that patients who take it must undergo blood tests every few weeks.

3. Plaquenil (Hydroxychloroquine)

This is a drug that was originally used in the treatment of malaria, but has been proven effective in rheumatoid arthritis. The drug is liable to affect the optic nerve so patients must be examined by an eye specialist once every six months. The drug is taken orally.

4. Methotrexate

This is one of the most effective drugs for the treatment of rheumatoid arthritis. It is given orally or by injection, once a week. Its main adverse effect, apart from common ones like nausea, vomiting and abdominal pain, is liver damage, so that patients who take it must undergo blood tests, including liver function tests, every few weeks. Impairment of liver function tests necessitate a halt in the treatment until the liver function tests return to normal. The drug is also liable to damage the bone marrow and suppress the production of blood cells such as red blood cells, white blood cells and platelets.

5. Arava (Leflunomide)

Leflunomide is a newer drug that has a similar mechanism of action to methotrexate. It, too, is liable to cause liver damage and must be used with the same precautions as methotrexate. It can be taken together with the latter.

6. Imuran (Azathioprine)

An effective drug, given in the form of tablets, that works by suppressing the immune system. This drug is liable to cause bone marrow suppression so blood tests have to be conducted regularly.

7. Cyclosporine and cyclophosphamide

Both of these are considered effective drugs, but both also suppress the immune system, so that treatment with them requires a close regular follow-up, including blood tests. They can also cause severe adverse effects in a number of systems, especially bone marrow suppression, severe infections, kidney damage, etc.

8. Antibiotics: minocycline

Although there is no proof that rheumatoid arthritis is caused by bacteria some patients show improvement after a number of months of treatment with antibiotics. One of the unique adverse effects is blackening of the skin. This change occurs mainly after exposure to sunlight so that prolonged periods of exposure to the sun are prohibited.

Treatment with disease-modifying anti-rheumatic drugs generally continues for many years. It is important to be aware of the fact that weeks and even months may pass before these drugs begin to work and show a beneficial effect. Normally, the effectiveness of these drugs decreases over time and they have to be replaced by other drugs from the same group. Today, patients are commonly treated with two or even three drugs at the same time in order to attain remission as quickly as possible.

Steroids

Steroids are hormones produced by the adrenal glands – two glands located near the upper poles of the kidneys. The hormones regularly secreted by these glands, including cortisone, are of the utmost importance since without them life cannot be sustained. They are among the body's most effective natural substances for the suppression of inflammation, so it is no wonder that drugs identical in composition have an impressive and even decisive anti-inflammatory effect. These drugs are given in the form of tablets or intramuscular or intravenous injections, or even directly into the affected joint. When the drug is injected into an inflamed joint its beneficial effect is felt within a few days. The drug must not be injected into the same joint more than 3-4 times in a given year. Injection of the drug does not usually entail serious adverse effects. Care must be taken to ensure that the injection is sterile in order to prevent bacterial infection in the joint. In light of their positive effect, steroids can be included in the group of disease-modifying anti-rheumatic drugs. Long-term use of these drugs may cause adverse effects so that they should be given in the lowest dose and for the shortest period of time possible.

New Drugs in the Group of Disease-modifying Anti-rheumatic Drugs

In recent years, several new drugs have been introduced that are now considered most effective in the treatment of rheumatoid arthritis. These drugs work by blocking the activity of proteins called cytokines. Under normal conditions there are two types of cytokines. One type is pro-inflammatory (promotes inflammation) and the second is anti-inflammatory (reduces inflammation). In health there is state of equilibrium between these two types of cytokines. In disease states this balance is upset. The pro-inflammatory proteins cytokines are produced in above normal quantities in patients with rheumatoid arthritis. Infliximab (Remicaide), etanercept (Enbrel) and adalimumab (Humira) are currently used in Israel and other drugs, already in widespread use elsewhere in the world, will be introduced in the future. While these drugs have been included in the national "basket of drugs," they are very expensive and therefore their use is approved in Israel only when treatment with the DMARD of the older generation, such as methotrexate and others, has failed. These drugs also have adverse effects that are liable to result in the development of severe adverse effects, including infections such as tuberculosis.

The Treatment of Rheumatoid Arthritis at the Dead Sea

In the mid-1980s, a group of rheumatologists headed by Prof. Shaul Sukenik of the Soroka University Medical Center in Beer Sheva began to study the effect of various treatments at the Dead Sea on patients suffering from rheumatoid arthritis. Forty patients were recruited for the first study and randomly allocated to four groups of ten each. The patients in the first group were treated with daily mud packs applied to all parts of the body. Patients in the second group were treated with daily baths in the hot springs waters. Patients in the third group were treated by a combination of these two treatments and the fourth group simply resided in the area, without receiving treatment of any kind. The fourth group served as a control group, since, as stated above, vacation and rest in a hotel far from the daily travails of life reduce stress and have a beneficial effect on arthritis. The treatment lasted for two weeks and the patients were examined by the same doctor at four different times: several days before they came to the Dead Sea, immediately upon completion of their treatment, and one and three months later. The examining physician did not know, of course, which treatment the patient he was examining had received. For each examination, a number of parameters were assessed that are generally used to determine disease severity including, among others, the number of inflamed and swollen joints, the power the patient could apply in making a fist (measured by a special instrument), the duration of morning stiffness in minutes and the maximum speed at which a patient could walk a distance of fifteen meters. In addition, several laboratory parameters were examined, such as the erythrocyte sedimentation rate, blood count, level of rheumatoid factor in the blood, etc. It is important to note that throughout the treatment and the subsequent follow-up period the patients continued to receive their usual drug therapy, with no change in the dose.

The results of this study showed a significant improvement in the condition of most of the patients in the three treatment groups, in most of the clinical parameters examined. This improvement continued, in most of the parameters, at least to the end of the follow-up period, three months after the treatment was concluded. In contrast to the improvement observed in patients in the three treatment groups, no significant improvement was seen in patients of the control group, who received no treatment at all. It is interesting to note that the clinical improvement was not accompanied by a corresponding improvement in the laboratory tests. This lack of correlation of clinical and laboratory improvement is a well-known finding that has been reported frequently by other research groups. In this study, the patients were not permitted to bathe in the Dead Sea and only the efficacy of treatment with hot mineral springs water, mud packs and a combination of the two was evaluated. Interestingly, we did not find any significant difference in the results of treatment in the three groups and so were unable to establish which of the treatments is preferable.

As mentioned, the patients in the first study were not permitted to bathe in the Dead Sea and so in the second study we decided to study the efficacy of bathing in the Dead Sea in comparison with bathing in the hot springs water. In this study as well the patients were randomly allocated to four groups: one group was treated by daily bathing in the Dead Sea, the second group by bathing in the hot springs water, and the third by a combination of the two treatments. Patients in the fourth group served as a control group, receiving no treatment at all. The treatment period again was two weeks and the follow-up period was three months. The study results showed that the efficacy of treatment by bathing in the Dead Sea was identical to that of bathing in the hot springs. The combination of the two treatments did not produce better results than either of the two treatments separately.

As mentioned above, the unique climate of the Dead Sea region has a beneficial effect on patients suffering from joint pain so it is possible that the climate influenced the results of the first two studies. To neutralize the beneficial effect on the results of these studies, the investigators from Soroka University Medical Center decided to conduct two clinical trials in Beer Sheva, which is at sea level. The first of these two trials investigated the efficacy of treatment with salt from the Dead Sea compared with regular table salt, which is comprised mainly of NaCl and is poor in trace elements and other salts, in comparison with Dead Sea salt. The patients recruited for this study were treated at home with one of the two types of salt. Neither the patients nor the treating physician knew which of the salts was used in each case, since the salt arrived at the patients' houses in packages that were identical in appearance and weight. The treatment lasted for two weeks. The patients were instructed to dissolve one package of salt in each bath and to assure, by means of thermometers, that the water was heated to a temperature of 35°C (95°F). The results of this study showed improvement in the condition of patients who bathed in

Dead Sea salt, but the improvement was less than that observed in patients treated at the Dead Sea area itself. The conclusion was that both the special climate and the restful environment, in addition to the mud and water, had a beneficial effect on the patients. For this reason, treatments offered at hotels located in big cities that call themselves spas and health resorts, but have neither the unique climatic conditions nor the special atmosphere of a health resort, are less effective than those provided in the Dead Sea area.

Another study, also conducted in Beer Sheva, investigated the efficacy of real Dead Sea mud in comparison with "fake" mud that had lost most of the minerals and trace elements that the real mud contained, as a result of repeated rinsing with regular tap water. This study showed that a significant improvement occurred in the condition of patents treated with real mud only and no improvement was observed in patients treated with the "fake" mud. In this study, too, the results were less impressive than those observed in patients treated at the Dead Sea.

The studies described above show, in a similar manner, that treatments at the Dead Sea including mud packs, bathing in the Dead Sea or the area's hot spring waters, or combinations of these treatments, lead to a significant, although temporary, improvement in the condition of most patients with rheumatoid arthritis. However, the follow-up lasted only for three months and laboratory results did not demonstrate a corresponding improvement.

These studies are very important because until their results became known the most famous European health resorts refused to allow patients whose condition was described as "severe and active" to receive treatments of this kind. The reason for this prohibition was the conviction that the treatments could make the patients' condition even worse, so that they should be recommended only when the condition of the patients was no longer considered to be active. To our regret a sizable number of health resorts still maintain these unwarranted restrictions. An additional advantage of the treatments is the lack of any severe adverse effects such as those frequently observed in treatments based on the administration of drugs. At the same time, it is important to understand that treatments at the health resorts do not cure patients with rheumatoid arthritis, but only provide a temporary improvement in their condition and in their quality of life.

b) Psoriatic Arthritis

Psoriasis is a very common skin disease that will be described in more detail in the chapter on skin diseases. Some psoriasis patients develop a particular joint disease that is different from that of rheumatoid arthritis. This disease is called psoriatic arthritis. The prevalence of this type of psoriasis-associated arthritis is approximately 0.1%, less than that of rheumatoid arthritis (1-2%). A definitive diagnosis of this special kind of arthritis requires the presence of the skin disease (psoriasis). In most cases the skin disease appears before the arthritis, occasionally as much as decades earlier. In a minority of cases the skin and joint diseases appear simultaneously. In even fewer cases the arthritis appears before the psoriasis and in those cases, of course, we cannot diagnose it as a case of psoriatic arthritis with certainty.

We differentiate between a few types of psoriatic arthritis:
▶ The most common type involves a relatively small number of small and large joints, generally in an asymmetric pattern. For example: left knee, right ankle and one finger.

Other, even rarer, forms of joint involvement are:
▶ Arthritis of all or some distal joints of the fingers and toes.
▶ Arthritis of many large and small joints in a symmetrical

pattern similar to that of rheumatoid arthritis.

► An asymmetric involvement of a few joints characterized by massive destruction of the affected joints, even to the point where they completely disappear.

► Injury to the entire spine, or parts of it, with or without involvement of the peripheral joints. This injury is somewhat similar to that seen in cases of ankylosing spondylitis. In these cases involvement of the peripheral joint is the consequence of inflammation of the synovia (synovitis) and the spinal involvement is due to inflammation at the site where ligaments or tendons attach to bone (enthesitis).

In psoriatic arthritis, tendons may be damaged because they are also partially covered by synovial tissue. One of the characteristic findings of this disease is the development of inflammation that involves all of the tendons, ligaments and joints of a single finger, or of a number of fingers and toes, that distorts the affected organ into the shape of a "sausage." This phenomenon is called dactylitis. Psoriatic arthritis can also affect other organs and tissues such as the heart, lungs and eyes. The severity of skin involvement is not always proportional to that of the joints. In some cases skin involvement is very mild, even to the point where the patient is unaware of its existence, or where the patient cannot see the lesion, as in involvement of the scalp or the backside. In these cases as well, which as stated involve the skin to only a mild degree, arthritis can be severe and widespread. For this reason, in all cases of arthritis of unknown cause patients must be examined from head to toe so as not to miss this diagnosis.

Psoriasis can also affect nails. This lesion can take on different forms, sometimes appearing like a nail fungus. In some patients, damage to the nails looks like many small pits in several nails, as if they had been jabbed with a needle. Normally, we are unable to predict which patients will develop psoriatic arthritis in the future, but apparently the chances are greater among patients who have these "holes" in their nails.

As with rheumatoid arthritis patients, psoriatic arthritis patients may develop severe deformities of the joints that can lead to severe crippling and significant impairment of their quality of life. Occasionally, psoriatic arthritis progresses even more quickly than rheumatoid arthritis.

Drug Therapy

The skin and joint lesions are not always correlated, but improvement in the condition of the skin is accompanied, at times, by improvement in the joints so patients should be treated by both a dermatologist and a rheumatologist.

Drug therapy is similar to that used in cases of rheumatoid arthritis. Here, too, we treat the pain with painkillers, including simple drugs, NSAIDs, Cox 2 inhibitors and others. On rare occasions these drugs may exacerbate the skin disease, so that the patient may end up "losing" in the end.

There are drugs for psoriatic arthritis that can change the course of the disease. Up to a few years ago the most effective drug in this group was Methotrexate, which is still very widely used. This drug has a beneficial effect on both the skin and the joints. Other effective drugs in this group are salazopyrine, imuran, plaquenil and others. In fact, this kind of arthritis can be treated with most of the drugs described in the chapter on treatment of rheumatoid arthritis.

The most important breakthrough in drug therapy for both psoriasis and psoriatic arthritis was the introduction of TNF Alpha antagonists, such as infliximab, etanercept and adalimumab. These drugs are very effective in the treatment of both the skin disease and the arthritis and their efficacy even surpasses that attained in rheumatoid arthritis.

The injection of steroids into affected joints is also recommended in psoriatic arthritis, especially among patients with a small number of affected joints. Oral administration of steroids is not recommended, except in severe cases, and only after all other forms of treatment have failed.

The Treatment of Psoriatic Arthritis at the Dead Sea

Unlike the treatment of psoriasis patients at the Dead Sea, which has proved effective in a great many studies, the effect of the Dead Sea on patients wih psoriatic arthritis has been evaluated in only a small number of studies. The first major study, which was conducted and published in 1991, showed that the treatments were effective, but to a lesser degree than for the skin disease.

This study, which was conducted by investigators from the Soroka University Medical Center, included 166 psoriatic arthritis patients who were allocated at random into two groups. The treatment of patients in the first group included daily bathing in the Dead Sea and exposure to solar radiation, while patients in the second group were treated with mud packs and bathing in the hot springs, in addition to bathing in the Dead Sea and exposure to solar radiation. The study lasted three weeks, during which all of the patients continued to take all of their regular drugs, with no change in dose. The patients who were treated with mud packs and bathing in the hot spring pools in addition to bathing in the Dead Sea and exposure to solar radiation showed a very significant improvement, especially in reduction of pain and increased range of movement in those parts of the back affected by psoriatic arthritis. In contrast, a similar impressive improvement of more than 90% was observed in the skin condition, with or without the addition of mud packs and bathing in the hot spring pools. The patients participating in the study were Germans who came to the Dead Sea for treatment at the expense of German medical insurance companies, so the effect of treatment after the patients left Israel could not be monitored.

A later study conducted by a different group of investigators from Ichilov Sourasky Medical Center, which was similar in plan and implementation to the previous study, and in which Israeli patients participated, showed that the beneficial effect on psoriatic arthritis can last for as long as six months.

Some psoriatic and rheumatoid arthritis patients also suffer from another disease: fibromyalgia, which is a non-inflammatory joint disease. A group of patients with both fibromyalgia and psoriatic arthritis, who were treated at the Dead Sea with mud packs and hot spring water baths in addition to exposure to solar radiation and bathing in the Dead Sea showed a significant improvement in the symptoms of both diseases. Interestingly, no correlation was detected between the improvements observed in the two diseases, so improvement in one disease did not necessarily result in a corresponding improvement in the other.

c) Ankylosing Spondylitis

The term ankylosing spondylitis comes from ancient Greek and means curved or bent spine. The disease primarily affects the spine, but can also affect peripheral joints. Inflammation of the sacroiliac joints that connect the pelvic bones to the spine must be present to make a definitive diagnose of this disease.

Unlike other diseases, this disease has been known for thousands of years. A visitor to the London Museum of Natural History or the Metropolitan Museum in New York can detect its signs in the sacroiliac joint in some of the ancient Egyptian Pharaohs, which can be seen clearly in x-rays of the mummies that have been so amazingly preserved.

As mentioned, the disease can affect both the spine and the peripheral joints, but by different mechanisms. Injury to the spine is caused by the development of inflammation in the areas that connect the vertebrae to each other. There, the inflammatory process is called enthesitis, after the precise anatomical location where the tendons and ligaments are attached to the bones (enthesitis). The ligaments, which have a very flexible structure, slowly and progressively lose their flexibility, change their structure, and become rigid with a chemical composition similar to that of bone. The final result is impairment of the range of spinal mobility. In extreme cases, the spine is affected along its entire length, to the point where the patient is at times totally immobilized. In the most severe cases the spine becomes like a broomstick. Sometimes the "broomstick" ("bamboo spine") is straight, but sometimes it is very crooked, especially toward the front, so much so that patients' horizons become limited and they are unable to cross the street alone, because they cannot raise their heads enough to see the traffic lights. Because injury to the spinal column results from inflammation at the site where tendons and ligaments are attached to bone, other tendons and ligaments that are far removed from the spine may also be affected. Thus, inflammation may appear at times in tendons such as the "Achilles tendon" among others.

Injury to the joints, in contrast, is caused by inflammation of the synovial tissue (synovitis), as is found in rheumatoid arthritis, although for the most part it is less severe. Generally there is a tendency for involvement of the joints of the lower limbs such as the hips, knees, or toes. The injury is normally asymmetrical and the number of joints affected is usually smaller than that in rheumatoid arthritis.

The causes of this disease are unknown but, for the first time, a direct association has been proven between it and a specific gene located on a specific chromosome. On chromosome 6 there is an area called B27 in which a gene is located that is associated with this disease. Not everyone with this gene will develop the disease; the gene is found in 7% of the general white population, while the prevalence of the disease is only 0.1%. However, the chance that someone with this gene will develop the disease is 90-fold greater than that of someone who doesn't have it. The disease is far more common in males than females (approximately 3-4 fold) and it is also more severe in males. It appears for the most part in the second or third decade of life and only rarely after the age of forty.

The presenting complaint in most patients is low back pain. Back pains are commonplace at all ages and we frequently say humorously that we distinguish between two populations: those who already have back pain and those who will in the future. The back pain that is typical of ankylosing spondylitis is called "inflammatory back pain" and is different from the more common back pain that is called "mechanical back pain." Inflammatory back pain appears gradually, continues for an extended period of weeks, months or years, increases when the body is at rest and is relieved somewhat by physical activity. Typically, patients who suffer from inflammatory back pain feel worse in the morning immediately after getting up and they gradually feel better during the day and following physical activity. At night, the pains usually return. In contrast, in patients who suffer from mechanical back pains, such as from a slipped disc or an ill advised movement that causes contraction of the back muscles, the pain appears suddenly, continues for a few days for the most part, and then passes. This kind of pain decreases with rest and increases with physical activity, so the patients feel best when resting in bed, but feel pain immediately after getting up and beginning physical activity.

Like rheumatoid arthritis or psoriatic arthritis this disease is also considered systemic, that is the disease is liable to affect other systems such as the eyes, heart and lungs. Injury to the heart, which is rare, can destroy the aortic valve (the valve between the left ventricle and the aorta) or in the heart's electrical conduction system. On rare occasions it may even be necessary to replace the aortic valve or implant a pacemaker. Injury to the lungs can cause breathing difficulty and the development of respiratory insufficiency (an extremely rare injury).

The disease usually progresses slowly. There is no way of predicting the extent of its damage. It is noteworthy that after the age of 40-50 it ceases to be active and does not get any worse.

Diagnosis

Physical examination always reveals some degree of limitation, mild or severe, in the range of spinal mobility. This limitation is liable to appear only in certain areas of the spine – the cervical, thoracic or lumbar areas – or in several areas in combination. The peripheral joints are not always affected.

In contrast with other joints, the sacroiliac is a deep structure, so it isn't possible to evoke tenderness of the joint by palpation, and tenderness is an important and typical sign of inflammation. Thus, in order to know with certainty if the joint has been injured, it is necessary to use an imaging technique such as x-ray, bone scan, CT scan or MRI. Other indicators of injury in these joints are characteristic back pains that continue for more than three months and a significant limitation in spinal mobility.

Drug Therapy

Up until a few years ago, there were no effective drugs for the treatment of this disease. Treatment was based mainly on giving painkillers and NSAIDs. It is known that the daily practice of physical therapy exercises may slow the progress of the disease, so it is important that patients exercise regularly. The main importance of the drugs is their ability to relieve pain and thus enable patients to engage in physical therapy, which, as already mentioned, is of the utmost importance, as is smoking cessation.

The introduction of drugs that block activity of TNF Alpha (antagonists) has changed this situation completely. These drugs are now the most effective drugs for the treatment of this disease. To our delight they have recently been added to the Israeli national basket of medications for this indication in addition to rheumatoid arthritis and psoriatic arthritis.

The Treatment of Ankylosing Spondylitis at the Dead Sea

Twenty-eight patients were recruited for a single study conducted in 2004 at the Dead Sea by a group of researchers from Soroka University Medical Center. The patients were allocated at random into two groups: one group was treated with mud packs and bathed in hot springs, while the second control group bathed in pools with regular water. The treatment lasted two weeks and the patients continued to take all of their regular medications, without any change. The examining physician didn't know, of course, to which of the groups the patient he was examining belonged. The patients were examined a few days before they arrived at the Dead Sea, after two weeks (at the end of the treatment period), and one and three months after the end of the treatment period.

The results of this study were very interesting, since a significant improvement in the patients' condition was observed in both groups. The improvement manifested as decreased pain and an extended range of movement of the spine that lasted for as much as three months after completion of the treatment. Significant improvement was also observed in the quality of life of all patients, as determined by a widely-used questionnaire that was designed to assess various indicators of quality of life.

The results of the largest study of ankylosing spondylitis patients conducted to date in Europe were published in 2001. One hundred and twenty-one patients participated in the study and were allocated to three groups. One group was treated at a health resort in Austria, the second at a health resort in Germany and the third continued to receive physical therapy at home, not at a health resort. This report also showed significant improvement, but only in patients who were treated at the health resorts, in comparison with those who were treated with physical therapy only. The improvement lasted as long as 40 weeks after completion of the treatment. The treatments at both health resorts also proved to be cost-effective in comparison with other treatments. Two other studies, one conducted at the Dead Sea in 1995 by Prof. Tishler and Prof. Yaron of the Sourasky Medical Center in Tel Aviv and the other at a health resort in Tiberias in 2002 by Dr. Hashkes, showed that treatment with mud packs and bathing in spring water also leads to temporary improvement in patients' conditions.

d) Juvenile rheumatoid arthritis

Despite the similarity in names, this disease occurs in children only and is entirely different from that of adults. The disease is classified into three distinct forms:

a) a form that involves a small number of joints
(up to five) – pauciarthritis,

b) a form that involves a large number of joints (more than five) – polyarthritis,

c) a systemic form.

Pauciarthritis

This form is more common in childhood. The large joints such as the ankle, hip, knee, etc., are normally involved. The disease appears for the most part by the age of two or three and on rare occasions after the age of ten. One of the common complications is inflammation of one of the inner parts of the eyes called the uvea. A stay at the Dead Sea also helps in the treatment of this eye complication. This is the most common of the three forms, appearing in about 50% of all patients.

Polyarthritis

This form is more common in children and appears for the most part between the ages of two and five, but can also appear later, from ten to fourteen years of age. This is the second most common form of the disease, occurring in 30%-50% of cases and uveitis is also seen.

The systemic form

This form comprises only 10%-15% of all case of juvenile rheumatoid arthritis. In addition to injury to the joints, whose number is not fixed, fever, even extremely high fever, is a common occurrence, together with various types of skin rashes. The disease is also known as Still's disease.

It is important to stress that other rheumatic diseases that are not so typical in the pediatric group, such as psoriatic arthritis and ankylosing spondylitis, may also be found in children.

The Treatment of Juvenile Rheumatoid Arthritis at the Dead Sea

No prospective controlled studies of children suffering from one of these forms of juvenile rheumatoid arthritis have been reported, so the knowledge that has been gathered is based mainly on a relatively small number of children who came to the Dead Sea for treatment as individuals. As in adults, treatment of children is based on bathing in the Dead Sea and hot springs and the application of mud packs. A good response to treatment has been observed in children with the systemic form of the disease and in children whose disease is accompanied by uveitis. Of course, when treating small children they should not be allowed to bathe in the Dead Sea or in the hot springs without close escort and supervision, even to the point of having their parents or a physical therapist hold them to prevent the risks and adverse effects of bathing.

Non-inflammatory Arthritic Diseases

a) Osteoarthritis

Osteoarthritis is the most common joint disease. Its prevalence rises sharply with increasing age; about 50% of 65 year olds suffer from it, while the decisive majority of 75 year olds show x-ray changes characteristic of the disease, although these changes do not always necessarily cause pain. In contrast to prevailing public opinion the disease is not caused by the natural aging process of the joints and many old people, even very elderly people, do not have it. Above the age of 65, the disease is more prevalent among women than men, but the difference isn't great.

Several factors affect the development of this disease: a) repeated and continuous trauma or excessive stress on a particular joint (for example, the disease is more common in the shoulders of baseball players who throw the ball with great force, in the knees and hips of football/soccer players, in the ankles of ballet dancers and in the lower back of parachutists, etc.), b) obesity has been proven to be a factor that accelerates the disease in load-bearing joints, especially the knees and perhaps also the hips, c) various metabolic diseases such as diabetes, in which osteoarthritis is inordinately prevalent, d) joint trauma; any joint that has suffered from trauma in the past, for any reason whatever, is more liable to be stricken by osteoarthritis (for example, patients who underwent surgery at a young age to correct a meniscal tear in the knee are more likely to develop osteoarthritis at an advanced age than those who did not), e) instability of a joint also accelerates the appearance of the disease in old age (for example, people born with instability in the hip joint who are not properly treated in infancy will suffer from osteoarthritis of the hip in old age).

Apart from these factors, there seem to be genetic factors, not yet discovered or identified, that affect the speed with which the disease appears.

It is interesting to note that some joints tend to be affected by the disease more frequently than others, and some remain almost totally unaffected. The joints most commonly affected are the small joints of the hands, knees and hips, the big toe and the cervical, thoracic and lumbar vertebrae, the shoulders, and others. Other joints, such as the wrist, the joints that connect the fingers to the palm, and the toes (with the exception of the big toe) are less frequently affected.

The causes of osteoarthritis are unknown. It is considered a primary disease of cartilage, a tissue that has relatively few cells. The job of these cells, like other cells in the body, is to repair damage caused to the tissue and to renew it. Through the years the ability of the cartilage cells (chondrocytes), which are relatively few in number, to repair damage caused by constant wear and tear declines. The cartilage begins to wear out and become thinner, and in severe cases may even disappear altogether. As a result, the two bones of the joint rub against each other when in motion and severe limitation of joint movement and pain results. This wear and tear on the cartilage results in a kind of instability of the joint, which contributes to the accelerated creation of new bone at the joint margins where bone and cartilage come into contact. The new bone grows in the shape of projections (osteophytes) that cause pain and limit movement in the joint.

The characteristic symptoms of the disease include, among others, pain that increases during movement and decreases during periods of rest and stiffness in the affected joint. For example, a patient suffering from osteoarthritis of the knees will complain of stiffness and inability to get up after sitting for a prolonged period of time, for example after watching a movie or TV. In contrast to rheumatoid arthritis, this stiffness continues for only a relatively short time – up to a half hour. Frequently, patients notice a change in the shape of the affected joint that occurs as a result of the growth of osteophytes. Of course, changes in the weather are liable to affect the symptoms: cold, rainy, wet weather affects the pain negatively and increases its severity.

For the most part, there is no need for imaging procedures to diagnose the disease since physical examination is enough. X-rays show characteristic findings of narrowing of the joint space, the appearance of osteophytes, etc. It is very easy to differentiate on the basis of x-rays between osteoarthritis and inflammatory diseases such as rheumatoid arthritis and others. There is no need for special laboratory tests to diagnose the disease. All of the tests are usually normal because there is no inflammatory process. In contrast to rheumatoid arthritis this disease does not shorten life expectancy, but can cause great suffering and severe disability with a significant effect on quality of life.

Since there is no practical way yet of transplanting cartilage cells into the affected joint to accelerate its growth (this technique is still in its infancy), treatment today is not curative but is designed only to alleviate pain. Treatment is divided into pharmacological and non-pharmacological therapy.

Pharmacological Therapy

The main objective of pharmacological therapy is to relieve pain. Any drug that relieves pain is acceptable. It is preferable to begin with one of the simple, safe drugs that have few adverse effects (paracetamol, propoxyphene, dipyrone and similar drugs). Only if the response to the treatment is insufficient is the use of one of the NSAIDs (non-steroidal anti-inflammatory drugs) or one of the Cox-2 inhibitor drugs recommended. Other drugs, such as tramadol, which mainly affect the central nervous system, have also been found to be effective. The regular use of narcotic drugs is not recommended, for fear of addiction, and their use is justified only in a few cases of severe exacerbation of pain and even then for a short time only.

Apart from pain relievers, steroids can also be injected into an inflamed joint. As stated above, this is an effective treatment approach that can be repeated not more than several times a year in a given joint. Some orthopedists recommend the injection of various materials to relieve pain and improve joint mobility by improving the viscosity of the synovial fluid. This treatment approach is expensive and its effectiveness has not been proven in all studies.

In recent years, the use of non-drug food supplements has increased. These food supplements, which include chondroitin sulphate, glucosamine, among others, are better known by their commercial names (Megagluflex, for example). These are materials created by the cartilage cells for the purpose of repairing damage and renewing cartilage growth. In the case of osteoarthritis, the cartilage cells produce these materials in large quantities anyway, to accelerate repair of the cartilage. The aggressive advertising of these food supplements, for which the commercial companies that create and market them are responsible, is scandalous and deceives the public. They do not build or repair cartilage as the advertisers and manufacturers claim, but only relieve pain. While a previous study, published in 2001 in the prestigious medical journal *Lancet*, showed that they might possibly slow the process of wear and tear in the cartilage, they do not have the ability to build cartilage. At present, a large-scale study involving thousands of patients is under way in the United States and we will soon know if these food supplements actually have any effect on the growth of cartilage. Today, after the initial findings of this study have been published in the prestigious *New England Journal of Medicine*, their effectiveness as analgesics has been shown to be similar to that of Acamol. In severe cases, surgical procedures of different kinds are needed to bring relief to the patient and prevent unnecessary suffering, but we will not discuss these in detail here.

Non-pharmacological Therapy

These treatments are based mainly on various physical therapy treatments, including water treatments (hydrotherapy). Care must be taken to ensure that the patients continue with regular physical activity but at the same time refrain from excessive strain on the affected joint and other activities that might hurt it. Weight reduction is important only in the case of patients suffering from osteoarthritis of the knees.

Treatment of Osteoarthritis at The Dead Sea

The initial studies that showed that different treatments bring about relief to patients suffering from osteoarthritis were published at the end of the 1970s and the beginning of the 1980s. These studies, conducted by Dr. Israel Machtey, did not include a control group of patients who stayed at the Dead Sea without receiving treatment of any kind. Three hundred and fifty-six patients suffering from osteoarthritis of the knees or the lower back took part in the study and were treated by daily bathing in the Dead Sea and hot springs. During the course of the study, improvement was observed in the mobility of both the back and knees as well as in grip strength.

In a later study Dr. Machtey assessed the effectiveness of Dead Sea salts dissolved in a bath for the treatment of osteoarthritis. This study was conducted far from the Dead Sea in order to neutralize the beneficial effect of the region's climate. The study examined the efficacy of treatment with various concentrations of Dead Sea salts dissolved in a bath. It was found that concentrations of as much as 7.5% and as little as 2% were effective, while a still lower concentration of 0.5% was not. Another investigator, Dr. Peter Engel from Germany, also reported on the efficacy of Dead Sea water in the treatment of osteoarthritis of the knees and hips.

In 1995, a group of investigators from Soroka University Medical Center in Beer Sheva, headed by Prof. Shaul Sukenik, published another study that was conducted in Beer Sheva, in which 28 patients suffering from osteoarthritis of the knees took part. The patients were allocated at random to two groups of 14 patients each. One group of patients was treated with Dead Sea salts and the other group with regular table salt. The study was double blind, that is neither the patients nor the examining physician knew which type of salt was being used. The salt was delivered by messenger to the homes of the patients in bags of five kilograms each. Five kilograms of salt were used in each bath in order to assure that the salt solution concentration was identical to the Dead Sea. The treatment lasted two weeks and the same doctor examined all of the patients. Each patient was examined prior to treatment, immediately upon its conclusion and then one and three months later. The study showed that only the condition of those patients treated with Dead Sea salt improved, but for most of the parameters tested the improvement lasted no more than three months after the conclusion of the study. A similar study conducted at the Dead Sea by the same group of investigators from Soroka University Medical Center showed that when the treatment was given in the Dead Sea region the results were much better and the beneficial effect lasted longer up to three months.

A later study published by a group of investigators from Soroka University Medical Center involved 40 patients suffering from osteoarthritis of the knees. The patients were allocated at random into four groups of ten patients each. One group was treated with daily baths in hot spring water, the second was treated in Dead Sea water, patients in the third group bathed in hot spring water and Dead Sea water, and patients in the fourth group stayed in the hotel but didn't receive treatment of any kind. The treatment continued for two weeks. The study showed a similar degree of significant improvement in the three treatment groups, while the condition of the patients who were not treated showed only very slight improvement, which was not statistically significant. According to this study, the three types of treatment were found to be more or less equal in benefit, without a clear advantage for any one of the treatment types over the others. The observed improvement lasted for as long as three months for some of the parameters.

It is interesting to note that groups of investigators from Sourasky Medical Center in Tel Aviv who conducted similar studies at health resorts in the region of Tiberias also reported that different types of treatment involving bathing in hot spring water or mud packs were effective in the treatment of osteoarthritis of the knees or hips and that the beneficial effect lasted for as much as six months. Treatment with "fake" mud (mud that lost most of its minerals after repeated rinsing with water) or bathing in fresh water (instead of mineral water) was not effective.

Recently, the results of an interesting study conducted at the Hamei Yoav health resort were published. In this study patients suffering from osteoarthritis came to the health resort once a week for treatment without having to stay over at the hotel. The treatment was no less effective in these patients than in patients who stayed at the health resort for daily treatment. These results are very surprising. If they are confirmed by additional studies, many other patients will be able to enjoy these treatments without having to pay enormous sums to stay at spa hotels.

In summary, a wide range of treatments given at health resorts provide relief and improvement in the patient's condition, alleviate pain caused by the disease, and improve quality of life. These treatments do not replace medication, but often enable patients to reduce the dosage of their drugs.

b) Fibromyalgia

Fibromyalgia is a syndrome characterized primarily by chronic pain in the soft tissues such as muscles, tendons and ligaments, and less in the joints themselves. In fact, there is no evidence for the existence of an inflammatory process of any kind in the joints and the results of all laboratory tests and x-ray studies are normal. The patients look healthy and there is no apparent explanation for the pain. Some investigators believe that this is a syndrome with a psychological or psychosomatic background. The syndrome was first documented in the nineteenth century and today there are accepted diagnostic criteria.

The syndrome is ten times more common in women than men and appears in most cases between the ages of 20 and 55, although it has been diagnosed among children as well as in adults and even in the elderly. Its frequency increases with age: at 20, the prevalence is 2%, at 70 it is about 8%. In some of the cases it appears following trauma or a short acute illness such as a viral disease.

The main symptom of fibromyalgia is disseminated pain in the muscles of the back and limbs. In most cases, the pain is constant, although its intensity may change. Patients are normally unable to pinpoint the precise location of the pain or to determine if its source is in the muscles or the joints. Occasionally, patients complain of swelling in the joints, although physical examination does not show any indication of swelling or limited joint mobility. The pain is usually affected by the patient's emotional state and may increase under conditions of stress, or even with changes in the weather. Complaints of a burning sensation or "pins and needles" in the limbs are very common and extreme fatigue is also seen among patients. Other common complaints include abdominal pain, changes in bowel habits (typical of irritable bowel syndrome), a burning sensation on urination and urinary frequency and urgency, migraine headaches, mood changes, depression, impaired sexual function, palpitations, dryness of the mouth and mucus tissues, etc.

Patients typically complain of sleep disturbance. They have difficulty falling asleep or wake up several times during the night because of pain. Because they do not sleep enough they are constantly tired, so there is great similarity between fibromyalgia and the chronic fatigue syndrome ("Yuppie disease").

Doctors use accepted criteria to diagnose the disease. The two most important are a) chronic skeletal or muscular pain that continues for over three months and involves the upper and lower parts of the body, b) pain produced by pressure on specific points in the limbs, neck or back (not on the joints), "tender points." For a definitive diagnosis of fibromyalgia in suspect cases, 11 of 18 fixed tender points must be painful on application of pressure (see illustration). Naturally, pain can be produced in anybody when pressure is applied even if they don't have the syndrome, and the appearance of pain depends on the amount of pressure exerted on the point. In patients with fibromyalgia pain is felt even after application of very slight pressure that would not cause pain in a healthy individual. It has been determined that the appropriate amount or pressure that should be applied to test for pain is about four kilograms per square centimeter. This amount of pressure will not cause pain in a healthy person. The examiner uses the thumb to produce the pressure and learns from repeated experience how to produce the right amount of pressure. This can also be done with a simple device called a "dolorimeter" (an instrument for the measurement of pain intensity) with which a precise determination of the amount of pressure required to produce pain can be made.

Studies of sleep quality have shown that most patients sleep lightly and do not reach deep stages of sleep. As stated above, laboratory tests and x-ray studies are typically normal and sometimes patients undergo many expensive blood tests and unnecessary and harmful x-ray examinations before the correct diagnosis is reached. Fibromyalgia can appear as a distinct disease (primary fibromyalgia) or in patients suffering from other kinds of joint diseases (secondary fibromyalgia).

Conservative Therapy

Unfortunately, no effective treatment for fibromyalgia is available yet. In many cases patients seek the help of different specialists such as rheumatologists, orthopedic surgeons, psychiatrists, physical therapists and practitioners of complementary medicine. It is only natural that specialists recommend treatments they believe in, which are usually different from those recommended by specialists in other fields. As stated previously, no treatment is truly effective and in many cases the patient is very disappointed with the results. This disappointment, together with the frustration caused by the fact that the blood tests and x-rays do not yield positive findings, often leads to anger on the part of the patient toward the treating physician. Some rheumatologists joke that if a doctor diagnoses a patient with fibromyalgia and treats him for a long time without getting into a debate or even a real fight, the diagnosis is probably wrong... It is very important to explain the nature of the disorder to the patient, including the limitations of all drug treatments and the low odds, at best, of success. It is even more important to calm patients and reassure them that this is not a case of arthritis that could lead to distortion of the joints and irreversible damage.

Drug therapy includes a wide variety of drugs used to treat inflammation (even though there is no sign of inflammation) such as NSAIDs and analgesics such as paracetamol. In recent years new painkillers have been used that have a different mechanism of action, such as tramadol and others. The syndrome leads to a lowered threshold of pain as a result of a defect in the central nervous system whose exact nature has not yet been clarified, so that drugs that affect the nervous system have also been found to be effective in some cases. These include anti-depressant drugs such as amitriptyline, flavoxamine, sertraline, and many others. Some of these work through a mechanism that suppresses the production of serotonin. Serotonin is one of the important transmitters that are secreted from nerve endings in the central nervous system and subsequently affect the central nervous system itself. It affects important metabolic processes such as temperature control as well as emotional processes such as mood and depression. Low levels of this substance have frequently been found in patients with fibromyalgia. Different drugs, such as anti-depressants and others that raise the level of serotonin in the central nervous system, have been proven partially effective in the treatment of fibromyalgia. Various drugs used in the treatment of epilepsy have also been found effective to some degree. Some doctors treat patients with cortisone injections at painful points, but most investigators do not recommend this treatment, which has not been proven effective in controlled studies.

Non-pharmacological Therapy

Regular physical activity is very important and helpful in alleviating pain. It is sometimes difficult to persuade patients to begin physical exercise programs because in most cases the beginning of activity can, paradoxically, increase suffering and pain. For this reason, it is important to explain to the patient that the increased severity is only temporary and will disappear within a few weeks, after which the patient's condition will improve. Other treatments such as hypnosis, acupuncture or relaxation therapy by means of various treatment methods have been shown to be effective in only a few studies. The prognosis is, for the most part, not so bad and most patients can continue to lead normal lives, although it may be assumed that they will continue in the future to suffer from pain and fatigue and will not be completely cured of the disease.

Treatment of Fibromyalgia at the Dead Sea

A study conducted by investigators from Soroka University Medical Center and published in 2001 examined the effectiveness of treatments at the Dead Sea for 48 female patients suffering from fibromyalgia. The patients were divided into two groups of 24 each. The first group bathed daily in the Ein Gedi hot springs, while the second group only stayed in the region and didn't receive treatment of any kind. The treatment lasted for ten days. Patients in both groups showed significant improvement, as determined by reduction in the number of tender points, and the frequency and severity of various symptoms such as fatigue, pain, stiffness, headaches, sleep disturbance, depression, etc. The study was based on physical examination of the patients by a single investigator who didn't know, of course, to which group each patient belonged. The patients all filled out standard questionnaires that investigators use to evaluate the efficacy of therapy and quality of life. The patients were examined before they went to the Dead Sea region, at the end of the treatment period (after ten days of treatment) and both one month and three months from the end of the study. As stated previously, improvement was observed in both groups, although it was somewhat greater and lasted for a longer time in the treatment group. Another study based on these same patients proved, once again with the help of questionnaires, that the patients experienced significant improvement in quality of life.

Similar studies conducted subsequently at other health resorts, especially in Turkey and Hungary, showed findings similar to those obtained at the Dead Sea.

c) Low back pain

It is said in joking that the population is divided into two: those who suffer from low back pain already and those who will in the future... and in fact low back pain is a very common phenomenon. It is estimated that 80% of all adults will experience at least one attack of back pain in their lives. Back pains are the number one reason for absenteeism from work. The problem is liable to have economic ramifications, especially in industrial plants or factories that are based on physical labor. Some studies have shown that the prevalence of chronic low back pain is as high as 25% of all employees in certain factories in a given year and that back pain that lasts for at least two weeks occurs among 14% of the work force. The highest prevalence of back pain occurs between the ages of 20 and 40, but for the most part it is more severe among older people. Many people who suffer back pain are frustrated by the results of conventional medical therapy and turn to various branches of alternative medicine, such as chiropractics, acupuncture, massage therapy and, of course, hydrotherapy and balneotherapy.

Two main types of low back pain can be distinguished: low back pain caused by an inflammatory process and back pains resulting from mechanical causes.

Inflammatory Back Pain

Inflammatory back pains are caused by an inflammatory process that affects the lower back. As examples of the inflammatory process, we can mention back pain associated with ankylosing spondylitis or psoriatic arthritis. There are infectious diseases that can affect the lower back – for example, abscesses, but these have entirely different clinical presentations with completely different symptoms, typically including fever.

Mechanical Back Pain

Mechanical back pain constitutes approximately 90% of all back pain and is the most common cause of back pain, especially when it occurs suddenly. The reason for the occurrence of such pains is usually damage to the soft tissues near the vertebrae, especially muscles. Very often back pain appears after extreme, short, physical effort that causes the feeling of a muscle spasm.

Another common cause of back pains of this type is damage to vertebral discs (the cartilage between two vertebrae) such as a tear (slipped disc). Back pain of this kind may be accompanied by radiation of the pain to one limb, or a part of it, and sometimes to sensory changes or a feeling of weakness in the limb, impairment of sphincter control, etc. The reason for this is pressure exerted by the disc on adjacent nerves. A typical example of this kind of pain is the syndrome known as "sciatica," which is caused by "slipping" of the disc resulting in pressure on the nerve adjacent to the slipped disc. In such cases, pain that radiates to the buttocks and the back of the hip is typical, and also along parts of the calf. Naturally, we must always remember that back pain may have other, more serious and graver causes that must be considered and ruled out, such as various tumors in the vertebral area.

Usually it is not difficult to distinguish between inflammatory and mechanical back pain and a correct diagnosis can be reached after a brief conversation of only a few minutes. For the most part, mechanical back pain appears suddenly after a strenuous effort or incautious movement, lasts from a few days to 2-3 weeks, is relieved by rest and is exacerbated by physical effort. Patients usually feel well when resting, but in the morning when they get out of bed the pain returns. In contrast, inflammatory back pain appears gradually and does not recede after a number of weeks but continues for months and even years. In contrast to mechanical pain, inflammatory pain decreases during physical activity and increases when the body is at rest. For this reason most patients with inflammatory back pain report pain during rest, at night for example, but have difficulty getting up in the morning. However, as the day progresses their condition improves. The NSAID drugs are more effective in treating inflammatory back pain.

Several studies conducted in Europe, especially in France, showed that different kinds of treatment provided at health resorts, such as bathing in mineral water and mud packs, are more effective than regular physiotherapy. Fifty patients with chronic low back pain were treated at a French health resort for three weeks. The treatment resulted in significant improvement in the range of movement in the lumbar spine, a decrease in the severity of pain, reduced consumption of painkillers and better function in general. It is interesting to note that this improvement continued more than nine months after completion of the study. The experience accumulated in clinics treating patients at the Dead Sea shows that the condition of most of the patients, especially those with mechanical back pain that appeared not long before the treatment was provided, improved. Unfortunately, no prospective controlled studies have been conducted to date on patients suffering from non-inflammatory back pains. Most of the patients treated at the Dead Sea came to the area on their own initiative, and did not remain long enough to attain optimum results from the treatment.

To study the efficacy of Dead Sea mud for patients suffering mechanical low back pain, special mud packs were developed at the plant of Ahava, Ltd., a company that normally produces cosmetic products from natural resources. After the mud packs are heated (in a microwave oven, for example) they are applied to the back for 20 minutes a day. The great advantage in this is that the packs can be applied by patients at home and they do not leave the back muddy upon removal. Investigators from Soroka University Medical Center studied the effectiveness of these mud packs for patients suffering from chronic mechanical low back pain of more than three month's duration. A control group of patients who also suffered from this disease and with the same degree of severity was treated in similar manner with "sham" mud packs. The mud in these mud packs had lost much of its mineral content as a result of continuous rinsing. The study lasted three weeks and neither the patients not the investigating physician knew which kind of mud was contained in the mud packs given to them. Both groups showed considerable improvement, but the improvement was more significant in the group treated with the real mud. The improvement lasted for up to a month after completion of the treatment. It is quite likely that the improvement observed in the control group resulted from the warming effect of the mud packs.

Patients suffering from upper back pain resulting from problems in the soft tissue, or degenerative problems of the cervical spinal column or disc problems can also benefit from these treatments, but despite the large number of patients successfully treated at the Dead Sea, controlled studies have not yet been conducted in these cases.

D) Other Rheumatic and Orthopedic Diseases

The efficacy of various treatments at the Dead Sea has been studied and proven only for a small proportion of the rheumatic and orthopedic diseases. I have no doubt that in the not too distant future it will be proven that these treatments are effective for a broader range of diseases or other syndromes of the musculoskeletal system, including, for example, gout. This disease is characterized by the depositing of uric acid crystals in a particular joint, accompanied by an acute inflammatory process that causes severe pain that ends within a few days as the crystals dissolve and disappear. Since bathing in mineral water (water from the Dead Sea or mineral springs) increases the secretion of sodium and phosphorous, it is reasonable to assume that it also increases the secretion of uric acid in the urine and thus reduces the level of uric acid in the blood. The decreased quantity of uric acid in the blood can reduce or even stop the deposition of crystals in the joints and thus reduce the frequency and severity of attacks.

It is reasonable to assume that these treatments would also help to heal inflammation of the tendons, ligaments or muscles more quickly so that athletes suffering from various kind of injury to the muscles or tendons would heal sooner. It is also possible that recovery after various surgical operations or trauma (e.g., following traffic accidents) would also be quicker.

Osteoporosis

This disease is characterized by weakening of the bones and subsequent appearance of fractures that cause patients significant suffering and may even shorten their lives. Various calcium-containing salts give bones their strength. Weakening of the bones is caused by increased loss of calcium from the bone. There are many reasons for this loss of calcium in the bones, including lack of physical exercise, insufficient calcium in the diet, disturbances in the absorption of calcium by the digestive system, increased loss of calcium in urine, various genetic diseases, rheumatic diseases, endocrinological diseases, a deficiency in sex hormones, and various drugs, such as steroids. The disease is more common among women but can also affect men, although at a lower frequency and at a more advanced age. Almost any bone is liable to break as a result of this disease, with the possible exception of the facial and cranial bones. The bones that break most frequently are the forearm near the wrist, the vertebrae, the hips, and others. Fractures of the femur are characteristic of advanced age because of their different structure bone. These fractures are the most dangerous and are liable to lead to severe disability and even death as a result of various complications that occur because patients become bedridden. It should be emphasized that the bones can break even when they do not sustain a significant blow. A patient is likely to remain unaware of fractures in the vertebrae, for example, which may only be detected in a chest x-ray taken for entirely unrelated reasons. A definitive diagnosis requires a bone density test.

Vitamin A is produced in the skin from raw materials and turns into an active agent after undergoing changes in the liver and kidneys. It is required to ensure sufficient absorption of calcium by the digestive system. The raw material needed for creating vitamin D is found in the skin, and under the influence of the sun's rays it is converted to an active vitamin. When the amount of this vitamin in the blood is insufficient the absorption of calcium by the digestive system is impaired, which may result in the development of osteoporosis. A study of Norwegian patients conducted at the Dead Sea by the DMZ Clinic, headed by Dr. Marco Harari, showed that after the patients stayed at the Dead Sea for several weeks the level of vitamin D in their blood rose significantly, especially in those whose vitamin D level at the time of their arrival in the region was below normal. Of course, this significant increase in the level of vitamin D in the blood was not in itself enough to treat the disease, and the patients needed other special drugs to improve bone density and reduce the risk of bone fracture.

CHAPTER 6

Health Resorts Treatment of Skin Diseases

The efficacy of various treatments at the Dead Sea was first proved for skin diseases. At the end of the 1950's investigators from Hadassah Hospital in Jerusalem published scientific papers that showed that the condition of psoriasis patients staying at the Dead Sea for treatment, which included exposure to the sun's rays and daily bathing in the Dead Sea, improved to an astonishing degree and that this improvement could last for many months. Since then, tens of thousands of Israeli and foreign patients suffering not only from psoriasis but other skin diseases as well have been treated with impressive success.

a) Psoriasis

Psoriasis is a chronic, non-contagious skin disease characterized by red blemishes and white scales. The term "psoriasis" comes from the Greek word psora, which means itch. The disease is widespread and its prevalence in the general population ranges from 2%-4%. It affects the sexes equally and can appear at any age. In most cases it occurs between the ages of 20 and 40, although it can appear in infancy as well as among adults and the elderly.

The cause of the disease is unknown but it is assumed that it has a genetic background – people with a certain genetic makeup will develop it more readily than those who don't have these specific genes. The disease also tends to appear in families. In most cases it is not severe and patients are able to go on with their lives without any significant impairment. As explained previously, patients with arthritis in addition to the skin disease suffer the most. Aside from the genetic factors, environmental factors as well as emotional and behavioral factors are also important. It is well known, for instance, that smoking and alcohol consumption increase the risk of getting the disease and both emotional stress and physical trauma can also result in its occurrence; for this reason it is designated a psychosomatic disease. Various drugs and bacteria are also liable to bring on the disease, and it is well known that cells of the immune system are involved in its development.

Skin has an impressive capability of renewal and growth. It renews itself continuously so that "old cells" are replaced regularly and frequently by new "young cells." The skin cells of a healthy person are replaced once every 28 days on the average. In psoriasis patients the skin is replaced much more rapidly, approximately once every four days. This rapid turnover is caused by defects in certain immune system cells that have not yet been sufficiently identified. It is this rapid turnover that causes the appearance of erythema (redness) and scales, which are no more than an accumulation of old skin cells before they are shed. Various inflammatory cells also accumulate within the skin.

The primary symptom of the disease is itching, although in many cases there are no symptoms. A distinction is made among several different kinds of psoriasis:

1. Plaque psoriasis
2. Guttate psoriasis

3. Pustular psoriasis
4. Inverse psoriasis
5. Nail psoriasis

1. Plaque psoriasis

For the most part, this disease appears among young adults and takes the form of layers of plaques on the scalp, elbows, knees and back. The layers are red in color with sharp borders that separate them from healthy skin and silver-colored scales within them. They come in different sizes, from one centimeter to 10 centimeters or more. As a rule, patients do not suffer from itching. On occasion, small "pits," which do not cause pain, can be seen on the surface of the nails.

2. Guttate psoriasis

This disease is more common among younger people and generally appears suddenly in the form of circular (tear-shaped) lesions of up to one centimeter in diameter. They are more common on the back than on the limbs. The disease is liable to appear following a streptococcal throat infection.

3. Pustular psoriasis

This is the most severe form of psoriasis, which can cause complications resulting from secondary bacterial infection. This form is sometimes accompanied by fever, a general feeling of malaise and diarrhea. Some patients may have liver involvement.

4. Inverse psoriasis

This disease is generally hidden within the recesses of the skin, as in the armpits, groin, buttocks or beneath the breasts. It is called "inverse" because it occurs in places that are not usually characteristic of psoriasis sites.

5. Nail psoriasis

This type can appear in all forms of psoriasis and cause great suffering. Its appearance is similar to that of a fungal infection and a microscopic examination is sometimes needed to reach a definitive diagnosis. Drugs, infection and alcohol can exacerbate the condition. The disease is usually chronic and patients do not achieve a complete cure although there may be extended remissions. Physical examination is usually enough for the diagnosis, although in rare cases a skin biopsy may be needed to confirm it.

Drug Therapy

Although we are unable to affect a total cure we do have a broad range of drugs whose efficacy has been proven to one extent or another.

a) Topical (local) therapy

These treatments include, among others:

• Various ointments, including ointments containing different types and doses of steroidal hormones.

• Ointments that soften the skin and increase its moisture content.

• Tar ointment based on tar-like components in different concentrations.

• Diavonex ointment and other ointments that contain vitamin D derivatives.

b) Systemic therapy

• Methatraxate. This drug was mentioned above in the chapter on rheumatoid and psoriatic arthritis. It is also highly effective in healing the skin lesions.

• Retinoids. These are derivatives of vitamin A. They are usually reserved for severe cases.

• Cyclosporine. An effective drug for both the treatment of psoriasis and its associated arthritis.

• New drugs from the TNF Alpha antagonist group, mentioned above in the chapter on psoriatic arthritis. They include etanercept, infliximab, adalimumab, and others. These drugs are highly effective and are included in the national health basket.

c) Phototherapy

Phototherapy is treatment with ultraviolet rays. It is based on knowledge that natural ultraviolet radiation improves the condition of psoriasis patients and this is the reason for the spontaneous improvement observed in most patients during the summer months.

There are several treatment methods that are based on electrical instruments that create and emit ultraviolet rays at different wavelengths.

• Treatment based on exposure of the patient to ultraviolet B rays (UVB, wavelength 295-320 nanometers). This method is used primarily in severe cases involving large areas of skin. In these cases, tar ointment can also be used.

• Treatment based on exposure of the patient to UVB rays only, at a wavelength of 311 nanometers. This method was shown to be more effective, because these rays penetrate deeper into the skin and thus reduce the danger of sunburn.

• Treatment based on exposure of the patient to UVA (wavelength

320-400 nanometers), together with the administration of Psoralen, a material given orally or in a bath. Since this substance, which is similar in structure to the anticoagulant coumadin, increases penetration of the skin by ultraviolet rays, it can be given before the radiation therapy. The combined therapy is called PUVA. Because UVB has fewer adverse effects the combined treatment is used only if treatment with UVB alone fails.

Treatment of Psoriasis at the Dead Sea

Psoriasis is without doubt the first disease to have been studied comprehensively at the Dead Sea. To date, tens of thousands of psoriasis patients have been treated at the Dead Sea with very impressive success.

Back in 1959, two investigators from Hadassah Hospital showed that treatment with water from the Ein Zohar hot springs had a positive effect on psoriasis patients. Since then, many studies have been published and international congresses have been held, showing the efficacy of these treatments. Israeli patients have also participated in the studies, in addition to patients from various European countries. In one of the larger of the studies, conducted and published in 1985 by Dr. David Abeles and his team, 1,448 patients, most of them health tourists from abroad, took part. Following treatment, complete remission was seen in 58% of the patients and a significant improvement in another 30%. The treatment included exposure to the sun's rays that lasted six hours a day in addition to bathing in the Dead Sea for an hour a day. The improvement in the condition of patients from abroad was greater than that in the Israeli patients, thanks to their longer stay (approximately four weeks, on the average, compared to two weeks, on the average, respectively). Another study, designed and conducted in 1974 by the Danish dermatologists, Dr. Avrach and

Dr. Niordson, involved over 500 Danish patients who stayed at the Dead Sea for four weeks. In this study significant improvement or total disappearance of the skin lesions was observed in 94% of the patients. When the disease recurred months later, it was less severe in most patients.

The most effective response to treatment in all types of psoriasis is seen in cases of plaque and guttate psoriasis. The response in the other types is not as good and a longer treatment period is required to attain a significant improvement. Treatment at the Dead Sea is not recommended for pustular psoriasis and it may even make the symptoms worse. The average period of remission is 7-8 months.

The mechanisms that contribute to improvement in the patients' condition have not yet been clarified satisfactorily. The major affect can probably be attributed to the ultraviolet radiation unique to this region. As mentioned above, because the Dead Sea is located at the lowest spot on earth and the air above its surface is saturated with vapor as a result of high temperatures that cause the water to evaporate, the sun's ultraviolet rays are blocked to a greater extent at the Dead Sea than anywhere else. The percentage of rays blocked varies with their wavelength. UVB rays are blocked more than UVA rays. The amount of radiation that reaches the surface of the earth also changes in accordance with the month of the year; radiation is greater in the summer than in the winter. The clouds that cover the sky in the winter months increase the blockage of ultraviolet rays and reduce the amount of radiation that reaches the ground. Thus, it is necessary to stay outdoors longer in the winter than in the summer to achieve the same therapeutic effect.

In addition to ultraviolet radiation, bathing in the Dead Sea and in hot springs is also important. This significantly delays the division of skin cells, whose excessively rapid division and proliferation are characteristic of psoriasis. Various studies have shown that some of the salts and elements in the water penetrate the skin tissue after bathing and these, apparently, slow down the process of skin cell proliferation. Of all the salts found in the Dead Sea in high concentrations magnesium and bromine have the greatest effect on skin cells.

Another interesting study investigated the question of which kind of treatment was most effective, exposure to solar radiation or bathing in Dead Sea water. Patients in the study were allocated at random to three groups. One group was treated with bathing in Dead Sea water in a covered pool without going out into the sun. The second group was treated by exposure to the sun's rays up to three and a half hours a day. The third group was treated with a combination of these two treatments. The treatment period was four weeks. An improvement of 22.1% was observed in patients of the first group, who were treated by bathing in Dead Sea water in a covered pool only, compared with 79% of patients in the second group who were treated by exposure to solar radiation and 87% of patients who received the combined therapy. From these results it was concluded that heliotropic therapy (exposure to the sun) is more effective than bathing in Dead Sea water and the combination of the two treatment methods produces the best results. Another study, based on a relatively small number of patients, showed that the combination of Neotigason, a drug from the retinoid group, with balneotherapy at the Dead Sea resulted in a better and longer period of remission in psoriasis than each of these two treatments alone (an average of 7.3 months as a result of the combined therapy, compared with 3.4 months with each of the treatments separately).

Other studies have shown that psoriasis patients can be treated successfully at the Dead Sea in all months of the year, but the treatment is less effective in the winter months (December, January and February), so patients need to spend more time in the sun during these months.

Today, we can easily measure the amount of ultraviolet radiation to which the patient is exposed during his stay at the Dead Sea, so we can prevent potential exposure damage. Exposure is measured by a sticker placed on the patient's skin that changes color with the amount of accumulated radiation. The amount of radiation that penetrates the skin depends, naturally, on the color of the patient's skin. Skin types are divided into five categories, distinguished from each other by the quantity of melanin in the skin (the pigment that determines the skin color). The first type is characterized by total absence of this pigment so that the skin is completely white (a phenomenon known as albinism). The fifth type is characterized by the maximum amount of pigment (black skin color). The three intermediate types are distinguished one from the other by the amount of melanin contained in the skin. Of course, the amount of time that the skin needs to be exposed to the sun's rays to attain maximal treatment efficacy depends on skin type; the greater the amount of pigment, the longer the required exposure time. We can determine precisely the amount of time needed and for this purpose doctors use special tables developed on the basis of years of experience.

Accumulated experience has shown that fewer than three hours a day in the summer months, three hours in the spring, a little more than three hours in the fall and between three and six hours in the winter are sufficient in most cases. The daily exposure should be divided into two sessions: the first session in the early hours of the morning, when the sun is not too hot, and the second session in the late afternoon hours.

Before staying at the Dead Sea, patients should consult a dermatologist with respect to the regular drug therapy that they receive at home, because changes in drugs or in their dosage may cause deterioration in the patient's condition. Several days before going to the Dead Sea patients should start using an ointment that contains Salicyl, a substance that helps to remove plaques from areas affected by psoriasis such as the scalp. In most cases patients can only start to bathe in the Dead Sea a few days after arriving in the region. This waiting period is essential to enable open sores and deep fissures in the skin, which can cause excruciating pain when immersed in the salty Dead Sea water, to close. It is always preferable to bathe in the sea before exposure to the sun. Dead Sea water also helps to remove plaques and reinforce the action of the ointment. After bathing and before exposure to the sun's rays, the body should be rinsed with fresh water and an ointment such as Vaseline should be spread on the skin. It is important to use sunscreens, which should be spread on the areas of healthy skin, especially on the face and neck, to reduce the harmful effects of the radiation. The required time for exposure to the sun should be divided into two periods. The patient should bathe in the sea once in the morning and again in the afternoon. The length of exposure to the sun and the amount of time spent in the sea should be increased gradually. The time of day recommended for bathing is between 8:00 and 11:00 in the morning and 2:30 to 5:00 in the afternoon. The amount of time required to attain a maximum effect varies with the severity of the disease and the type of psoriasis involved. The shortest recommended period is two weeks, but in severe cases a longer period of four weeks or even more is required for the patient to get the maximum benefit from the treatment.

Even though the frequency of sunburns at the Dead Sea is the lowest in the world the risk still exists even there, so the duration of exposure to the sun should be increased gradually. It is noteworthy that the incidence of skin cancer such as melanoma is no higher in patients treated at the Dead Sea compared to patients not treated in the Dead Sea region. In contrast, an increase was observed in the frequency of solar keratosis, which is considered to be a pre-malignant lesion.

It is important to emphasize that the Dead Sea site is the only health resort in the world whose efficacy in treating psoriasis has been proven in many scientific studies published in the medical literature. At other resorts, including Spain and Yugoslavia, which also treat psoriasis patients, no convincing studies have been conducted and published concerning the efficacy of the treatments provided.

Most of the work published has shown that treatment with natural ultraviolet light gives better results than treatment with artificial ultraviolet light.

b) Vitiligo

Vitiligo is an acquired skin disease with a prevalence of 1% to 2% in the general population. It affects both sexes equally. The disease results from injury to certain cells (melanocytic cells) that produce melanin, the skin pigment. The cause of the disease is unknown. In most cases it appears in the third or fourth decade of life, but can occasionally appear at either a younger or an older age. It is almost certain that there is a genetic background that also contributes to the appearance of the disease, because in some instances more than one case is discovered in the same family. The affected areas appear as white, pigment-free stains, which vary in size and number.

Sometimes they are very extensive and their area may cover more than 50% of the total skin area. The affected area can be clearly distinguished by a sharp border between the sick and healthy skin areas. If hair grows in the affected areas it is not shed, but also turns white. The areas frequently affected occur around apertures such as the eyes, mouth, nose, the rectum, and the genitalia in addition to other areas on the limbs and across the back. The disease can affect mucosa such as oral mucosa (the internal lining of the mouth) and the retina (the lining at the back of the eye). The disease is usually progressive, although there is spontaneous regression in 10% to 20% of the cases. There is no way of knowing in which patients the disease will progress and in whom it will clear or at least recede.

Sometimes the disease appears in combination with other diseases that are considered to be autoimmune, that is, diseases of the immune system that affect different tissues and organs of our bodies for unknown reasons. For example, it can appear in patients suffering from diseases of the thyroid gland, from under-activity of the adrenal glands (two glands located next to the kidneys that produce various hormones such a cortisone), from regional baldness, a certain kind of anemia (lack of blood), etc. Conditions of tension and stress can increase the severity of the patient's condition. The disease is also liable to appear after exposure to various substances such as organic solvents.

Treatment

No effective treatment is known for this disease. The suffering is mainly psychological and stems from the esthetic damage.

The following conservative treatments are worthy of mention:

1. Ointments containing different concentrations of cortisone. This treatment is effective mainly in mild cases, where less than 10% of the total skin area is affected.

2. Systemic cortisone therapy. This treatment is required in cases where the damage is more severe and more widespread.

3. Ointments containing various materials such as Tacrolimus, which is also used following organ transplants to prevent rejection of the transplanted organ by the immune system.

4. Ultraviolet radiation. This treatment is recommended primarily in more severe cases. It is called PUVA therapy and is usually combined with the drug Psoralen in the form of an ointment, or taken orally as in the treatment of psoriasis.

5. Treatment by narrow band UVB radiation (around 311 nanometers).

6. Ointments containing the enzyme pseudocatalase, which is vital for the break down of products of oxygenation such as H2O2 that accumulate in the skin and impair the proper function of melanin-producing cells. Lower than normal quantities of this enzyme have been found in patients with vitiligo.

7. In especially severe cases, where most of the skin has been affected and no improvement is observed despite the treatments mentioned above, treatment can be tried with drugs that destroy melanin-producing cells that are still active in the healthy areas. This treatment will result in vitiligo over the entire skin area, and the skin will appear entirely white without patches.

Treatment of Vitiligo at the Dead Sea

Up until a short time ago, the treatment of vitiligo at the Dead Sea was based primarily on exposure of the patients to the special ultraviolet radiation in the region. To obtain maximum results the patients had to remain in the area at least four weeks and in many cases even more. The duration of exposure to the sun must be increased gradually and slowly in order to prevent radiation damage to the affected areas that do not contain melanin, the pigment that aside from being responsible for skin color also protects it from radiation damage. Sometimes the improvement becomes maximal only after the patients have left the region. A study conducted in the early 1990s showed that in 11% of the patients who remained in the area for between four and five weeks the damaged areas disappeared completely, or almost completely, while in 82% of the patients only partial improvement was observed. The longer the patient remained in the area, the greater the improvement.

Most of the patients lacked the pseudocatalase enzyme, which breaks down oxygenation products such as H_2O_2 that normally accumulate as a result of various metabolic processes and are liable to damage melanin-producing cells. An interesting study was conducted in 2002 by Dr. Harari of Israel and Dr. Schallreuter of Austria, which compared the efficacy of treatment by exposure of the patients to ultraviolet radiation at the Dead Sea with treatment that combined solar radiation and local, topical treatment with an ointment containing this enzyme. A third group of patients was treated by exposure to solar radiation and a "sham" ointment that looked like the real ointment but didn't contain any active ingredients. Skin concentrations of the toxic material H_2O_2 in the skin were measured and determined by a special method before and after the treatment (21 days after the start of the treatment). The study, in which 55 patients participated, was double blind so that neither the patients nor the examining physician knew which type of treatment was administered. Before the treatment began, high levels of H_2O_2 were found in all groups. The improvement observed was greater and occurred more rapidly in the group that received the combined treatment of radiation and real ointment than in the other two treatment groups. The treatments also resulted in a significant decrease in the level of toxic substance in the skin.

c) Atopic Dermatitis

Atopic dermatitis (inflammation of the skin) is a chronic inflammatory disease of the skin with an allergic and familial background. Patients who develop the disease sometimes suffer from other diseases such as asthma or allergic nasal drip as well. The disease is also known by other names such as "asthma of the skin" or "eczema". It is found in all ethnic groups and races. In the great majority of cases it appears before the age of five and is somewhat more common in girls than in boys. The disease is caused by a reaction of the immune system to an as yet unknown factor. Some patients are allergic to certain substances or foods, as is demonstrated by skin tests. In about 50% of patients there is more than one case of atopic dermatitis.

Clinical Symptoms

The main symptom is the appearance of red blemishes in the form of blotches on the skin that are generally accompanied by severe itching. On occasion, fluid-secreting blisters may appear. In chronic cases the skin is thickened with lumps that are mildly scaled. Children are affected mostly in the face, scalp, limbs and back, while areas such as the armpits, buttocks and groin are almost never affected. In adults the disease appears mainly on the neck, behind the knees, in the folds of the elbow and in other places such as the face, forearm, wrists, etc.

The diagnosis is clinical and for the most part it is unnecessary to do a biopsy. Chronic itching, a family history of similar cases and an age appropriate onset of disease are helpful in arriving at a diagnosis.

Treatment

First and foremost, patients should avoid or prevent exposure to things that are liable to increase the severity of their condition, such as excessive bathing, low humidity, rapid weather changes, dry skin, stressful circumstances and exposure to substances such as cleaning agents or solvents.

It is most important to assure a constant level of skin moisture. Dry skin can exacerbate the condition and increase the itching. Patients should use moisturizing agents that contain relatively little water and more oily materials to prevent the evaporation of large amounts of water that can lead to undesirable dryness of the skin. The agents should be spread on the skin several times a day, especially after bathing.

Treatment of the disease is based on drugs and especially ointments containing different concentrations of corticosteroids (like cortisone). Excessive use of these drugs should be avoided. It is usually enough to apply them once a day and not to use them continuously for a lengthy period of time. In cases of severe flare-ups, it is sometimes necessary to treat the patient with oral cortisone until the attack passes.

One of the causes of the itching is histamine, which is a protein compound that is produced by most of the body systems and stored in special cells called mast cells. The release of histamine by these cells causes different physiological reactions such as pain, dilatation of blood vessels, constriction of air passages and more. Histamine also plays an important role in allergic reactions such as allergic rhintis and reaction to insect bites. Increased secretion of histamine also causes itching, which sometimes is extremely troublesome to the patient. Treatment is based on the administration of antihistamines that block the production of histamine.

Relatively recent studies have shown that certain ointments containing materials such as cyclosporine or tacrolimus that affect the immune system are also beneficial.

As with psoriasis, this disease can be treated with ultraviolet radiation of the UVA, UVB, or narrow-band UVB type, or a combination of UVA with psoralen (PUVA therapy).

Treatment of Atopic Dermatitis at the Dead Sea

The treatment of atopic dermatitis at the Dead Sea, like treatment for psoriasis, is based on bathing in Dead Sea water and ultraviolet radiation. The results are usually very good, although somewhat less beneficial than in psoriasis. The improvement is usually slower and patients sometimes have to remain at the health resort for six weeks to attain maximum improvement. Relief from itching usually precedes improvement in the skin lesions. The best treatment results are observed in the spring or fall. Total or almost total disappearance of the skin lesions and itching can be achieved in two-thirds of the patients if they remain at the Dead Sea for six weeks. After a stay of four weeks or less only 50% of the patients achieve remission. During their stay at the Dead Sea the patients must continue to lubricate their skin and keep it moist by applying suitable ointments and creams, especially immediately after bathing.

German investigators have shown that atopic dermatitis patients can also be treated far from the Dead Sea region. The treatment combines immersion of the patient in a bath containing a 10% concentration of Dead Sea salts dissolved in fresh water and narrow-band UVB ultraviolet radiation given to the patients while they are in the bath. The treatment is repeated several times a week, with the exposure period varying by skin type. Patients with fair skin require a shorter exposure time than those with dark skin. This artificial treatment is somewhat less effective than that of natural treatment and, of course, far more expensive.

A study conducted by the German Dr. Proksch and his colleagues in 2005 on atopic dermatitis patients investigated the effect of a 5% concentration of Dead Sea salts dissolved in a bath. The study was designed as follows: each patient immersed one forearm in a bath containing the dissolved Dead Sea salts and the other forearm in a bath of fresh water. Each treatment lasted 15 minutes and was given daily for six weeks. During the course of this study the patients were not treated by ultraviolet radiation. Before the start of the study and after its conclusion various parameters were examined, such as loss of water through the skin, moisture level, and roughness and redness of the skin. The results of the study showed that only in the arm treated with Dead Sea salts was there a reduction in water loss from the dermis with a resulting increase in its moisture level. Similarly, decreased roughness and redness of the skin (symptoms of the inflammatory process) were seen only in the arm bathed in the Dead Sea solution. It is assumed that the main cause of improved function in the diseased skin is the magnesium salt found in large quantities in Dead Sea water. Magnesium plays many roles that are vital for the functioning of the immune system, and a shortage of this element is common to many of the autoimmune diseases. Magnesium and magnesium salts block penetration of skin tissue by various substances, including toxic materials. Thanks to their ability to attract water molecules they also increase the level of moisture in the skin, which is vital for its proper function.

d) Treatment of other Skin Diseases at the Dead Sea

There are other skin diseases that apparently can be treated at the Dead Sea, but controlled studies have not yet been conducted to prove their efficacy and there is insufficient experience to date to recommend them. The following is a brief summary of these diseases.

Mycosis Fungoids

This disease is manifested as tumors of the skin's immune system cells. These cells, called T-lymphocytes, are liable to cause different kinds of immune system tumors if they do not function properly. This is a rare kind of tumor with an incidence rate of only three cases a year per million population. The skin manifestations of the tumor, which occasionally includes itching, can be very similar to that of other diseases, such as psoriasis or eczema, so that in most cases the precise diagnosis is delayed. The exact diagnosis requires a biopsy of the involved skin. We usually distinguish between disease stages based on the severity as seen in the biopsy. In the early stages, when it is limited to the skin, the prognosis is excellent and the disease does not result in reduced life expectancy. In rare cases, the disease spreads beyond the skin to other organs and tissues, in which case the prognosis is not as good. In most cases the disease does not affect other tissues but remains localized to the skin.

Experience based on a relatively small number of cases has shown that treatment at the Dead Sea (bathing in Dead Sea water and exposure to its solar radiation) improves the condition of patients suffering from this disease in its early stage. There is no proof that the treatment is effective for patients in whom the disease has already reached an advanced stage.

Ichthyosis

This is a group of diseases characterized by dry skin and itching that may sometimes cause extreme discomfort and may last for a long time, with significant thickening of the skin's keratin layer. The primary treatment is based on constant lubrication of the skin using various preparations. It has been proven that bathing in Dead Sea water also affects the keratin layer, which loses some of its thickness and becomes somewhat more moist and supple.

Patients suffering from other skin diseases have also been treated successfully at the Dead Sea, but in the absence of controlled studies involving a sufficient number of patients it is not yet possible to recommend these treatments. Among these diseases we can mention itching from various causes – Lichen Planus, Acne Vulgaris, Morphea and other, rarer diseases that will not be described here.

CHAPTER 7

Health Resorts for the Treatment of Lung Diseases

Staying at the Dead Sea region has a positive effect on patients suffering from chronic lung diseases among adults and children, such as chronic obstructive pulmonary disease (COPD), cystic fibrosis, asthma and others.

a) Chronic Obstructive Pulmonary Disease (COPD)

COPD is the fifth most common cause of mortality in the world and it is assumed that its rate will only increase in the future. The disease is characterized by an irreversible impairment or obstruction to airflow in the respiratory tract. This disease includes several syndromes, the primary being pulmonary emphysema and chronic bronchitis. Emphysema is characterized by irreversible damage to pulmonary alveoli – small air spaces in which exchange of gas takes place. Chronic bronchitis is characterized by inflammation of the small air passages accompanied by a permanent cough and the production of large quantities of mucus that adds to the obstruction of air passages. The disease is more common among adults over 50, but can also appear at a younger age. It is most common among men. As a result of the obstruction of air passages and the impairment of gas exchange in the lungs, the amount of oxygen transported to the body tissues declines (hypoxemia), resulting in a surplus of carbon dioxide (hypercarbia). This can be followed by the development of pulmonary hypertension that causes right sided congestive heart failure manifested primarily by swelling (edema) in the lower limbs and increasing shortness of breath until, in extreme cases, the patient is unable to make even the slightest effort. This is considered to be a multisystem disease that can causes significant weight loss, weakness, muscle wasting and significantly lowered life expectancy.

The main cause of COPD is smoking. German doctors who worked under the Nazi regime at the end of the 1930s and during the 1940s were the first to report on the association between smoking and lung cancer. Even way back then, they conducted an aggressive campaign against smoking, including smoking in public places, and took pride in the fact that the exceptional stamina of their leader, Adolf Hitler, stemmed from the fact that he neither smoked nor drank alcoholic drinks, in contrast with the leaders of the countries they were fighting, including Churchill, Stalin and Roosevelt. Only at the end of the 1950s did the first prospective studies begin to appear in the United States, reporting on the direct relationship between an increase in the number of cigarettes smoked and a decline in lung function, and the rapidity with which damage was incurred. Approximately 20% of all smokers will develop the disease over time. It is almost certain that some of the substances exhaled in cigarette smoke injure and possibly even destroy the cells lining the air passages, whose physiological function is to assist in the removal of mucus and toxic substances from the lungs. Another risk factor for the disease is an inherited deficiency in the Alpha-1 antitripsin enzyme. This enzyme is needed to neutralize the activity of various substances such as those secreted by the white blood cells that accumulate in the lungs in cases of inflammation and cause damage to lung tissue. Lack of this enzyme causes the substances to destroy the pulmonary alveoli. Air pollution, too, which is typical of urban areas, has a significant effect on the development of the disease, which is in fact more common in urban than in rural areas. Employees in certain industrial plants, such as the cement industry, mines, the rubber industry, etc., tend to became ill more frequently with this disease as a result of their exposure to toxic substances.

As stated above, the disease is caused by constriction of the air passages that impairs the exchange of gas in the lungs, causing irreparable damage. The first sign of impairment of gas exchange is a decrease in the level of oxygen in the blood and, at a later stage, accumulation of carbon dioxide in the blood. Clinically, the main sign is shortness of breath that in the beginning only appears after physical effort, but at later stages of the disease also appears after the slightest effort or even at rest. Typically the patient breathes more rapidly or with greater effort. The patient uses auxiliary muscles to assist breathing, such as those around the nostrils and the mouth, which in normal circumstances are not used for breathing. Patients sometimes become "barrel-chested", which is characteristic of the disease, and in different cases cyanosis (blue-coloring in the skin) is also seen around the face and fingertips.

We rely mainly on lung function tests to diagnose COPD. The lungs of a healthy non-smoker reach peak capacity and functionality by the age of 25. The functional evaluation is based primarily on two indicators:

The first is the maximum volume of air exhaled in the first second, after the patient has filled his lungs with all the air they can hold. This indicator is called FEV-1: forced expiratory volume in one second. The FEV-1 in a healthy person of 25 is about four liters of air. After this age, it decreases gradually, but steadily. In smokers the decline is faster (2-5 times the normal rate). The severity of the disease is proportional to this index, that is the lower the FEV-1 the more severe the disease. Clinical symptoms appear when the FEV-1 decreases to two liters a second.

The second indicator is the maximum volume of air that the lungs can absorb. This indicator is called FVC – forced vital capacity. When the ratio between FEV-1 and FVC is smaller than 0.7 the disease can be diagnosed with certainty. The severity of the disease is also determined according to the value of FEV-1. The further it drops below the expected value the greater the severity of the disease. For example, when the FEV-1 is less than 30% of expected, the disease is considered to be extremely severe.

Treatment of the Disease

The most important and effective treatment is, of course, to stop smoking at any stage, even after many years of smoking, since smoking significantly accelerates the pace of deterioration in lung function. Patients must get all necessary vaccinations, especially a flu shot before the onset of winter, because all pulmonary infections affect these patients much more, and may even sometimes be life threatening. The patients must also be treated by physical therapists who can show them how to get rid of mucus most effectively and how to exercise their respiratory muscles. In cases of increasing severity, antibiotic therapy is required, especially when the exacerbation is known to be caused by infection. In the more severe cases, the patient may undergo an operation to remove parts of the lung that cause recurrent and severe infections, or even a lung transplant in the most severe cases when all other treatment methods have failed.

Drug Therapy

The main drug treatments are:

1. Drugs that dilate the air passages. These are taken by means of inhalers (the preferred method), by oral systemic administration, or sometimes by injection.

2. Steroids given by means of an inhaler, as tablets taken orally, or by injection.

3. Drugs that soften the mucus and facilitate expectoration.

4. Treatment with oxygen. This is the only treatment that has been proven to reduce mortality in COPD patients. The treatment is essential when the level of oxygen in the blood falls below 88%-90% at rest. Most patients need to receive oxygen for at least 12 hours a day and some must do so regularly and continuously.

**Treatment of Chronic Obstructive
Pulmonary Disease (COPD) at the Dead Sea**

Sir Richard Francis Barton, an investigator of diseases and a linguist, who lived in England in the 19th century, traveled to countries throughout the world in his search for an ideal location for curing pulmonary diseases, and especially tuberculosis, and was aware, even at that time, of the advantages of the Dead Sea climate. In his memoirs, written by his wife, he said: "I recommend taking advantage of the beautiful Dead Sea region situated 1,300 feet below sea level in a location where oxygen accumulates and you can run all you like without suffering shortness of breath." He proposed the construction of a hospital in the area, bigger than any built at that time, for the treatment of lung diseases – apparently for sufferers of tuberculosis, a disease that was most common at the time. Since those days, much knowledge and experience have been gathered that confirm his assumptions.

Treatment of COPD patients at the Dead Sea is in fact based

on the unique climatic conditions of the region, especially the barometric pressure that is the highest in the world, because the location is the lowest spot on earth.

The first study was published in 1994 by investigators from Hadassah Hospital in Jerusalem, headed by Prof. Kramer. Ten patients suffering from advanced-stage COPD, all of whom required supplemental oxygen therapy, participated in the study. Three were young people with cystic fibrosis, which is also a cause of COPD. All of the patients underwent a series of examinations several days before leaving Jerusalem, their permanent place of residence. This was followed by a second series of examinations six days after their arrival at the Dead Sea and a further two sets of examinations, one week and two weeks after their return to Jerusalem. The examinations included lung function testing, blood oxygen saturation, capacity to undertake strenuous physical activity, and blood oxygen saturation during sleep.

The difference in altitude between Jerusalem, situated at 800 meters (2,624 feet) above sea level, and the Dead Sea, located approximately 400 meters (1,312 feet) below sea level, is about 1,200 meters (3,937 feet). Accordingly, the barometric pressure at the Dead Sea is greater than that in Jerusalem: the barometric pressure at the Dead Sea is about 800 millimeters mercury (31.5 inches), while in Jerusalem it is about 691 millimeters (27.2 inches) mercury. It is also known that the higher the barometric pressure the greater the amount of oxygen concentrated in the air and the greater the amount of oxygen that reaches the pulmonary alveoli. A simple calculation shows that the pressure of oxygen in the lungs increases significantly at 22.8 millimeters (0.9 inches) mercury. Simply put, a patient at the Dead Sea benefits from the same therapeutic effect that he would experience by receiving oxygen from an oxygen balloon and mask delivered at the rate of one liter per minute.

The results of the study showed significant improvement in the patients' condition. The partial arterial oxygen pressure rose from an average of 51.6 mm mercury in Jerusalem to an average of 67 mm mercury at the Dead Sea. The partial carbon dioxide pressure (which must not be allowed to rise significantly) rose only slightly – from 43.2 mm mercury to 45.9 mm mercury. Blood oxygen saturation increased from 87.7% to 92.8%. Even the blood oxygen saturation during sleep improved, as did patients' exercise capacity and tissue exploitation of oxygen. All of the patients reported that they felt much better and needed to use oxygen much less, in contrast with the state in Jerusalem. These good outcomes disappeared very quickly once the patients were back in Jerusalem, perhaps because they had stayed at the Dead Sea for too short a period (only one week). In a later study conducted by the same group of investigators from Jerusalem headed by Prof. Kramer, published in 1998, eleven patients suffering from COPD stayed at the Dead Sea for a longer period of time – three weeks. The results of this study were similar to those of the first study. The improvement observed in the level of oxygen in the blood and in the pulmonary arteries disappeared immediately on their return to Jerusalem, but the improvement in their exercise capacity and their ability to use oxygen more efficiently lasted at least two weeks after they returned home. Further research is needed to determine whether longer stays at the Dead Sea will result in a more lasting therapeutic effect, even after the patients return home. There is no doubt that patients would prefer the help of natural oxygen from the Dead Sea region to being tied endlessly to an oxygen bottle that they have to carry with them at all times.

We will summarize this chapter by saying that, as Sir Richard Francis Barton believed, there is in fact enormous potential for the construction of a hospital, or at least a residential community, in the Dead Sea region for patients suffering from COPD.

b) Cystic Fibrosis

Cystic fibrosis is a hereditary disease that affects several vital systems, particularly the lungs. Its incidence in the general population is one case per 2,000-3,000 births. The overwhelming majority of cases are diagnosed in childhood, but a few cases, generally less severe, are diagnosed only in adolescence. In the not-too-distant past, cystic fibrosis patients died before reaching adolescence. Today, thanks to improved treatment methods and the possibility of lung transplant in very severe cases, almost 40% of all patients live to the age of 18 or even more. The average life expectancy of patients is approximately 30 years and some live much more.

This hereditary disease is caused by a change (mutation) in the structure of a gene on chromosome 7. Even though several systems are usually affected, most of the damage, illness and death are related to lung involvement. The major defect is in chlorine transport that causes a problem in the secretion and physiology of mucus, which becomes excessively thick. This defect causes accumulation of mucus in the lungs impairing their ventilation capacity. The consequence is frequent lung infection that over the course of time can result in increasing damage to the lung tissue, and ultimately in their terminal insufficiency.

As stated above, other systems are affected as well and in general most of the patients also suffer from sinusitis, which appears in early life. Another common defect is functional deficiency of the pancreas. This gland is vital for the breakdown and absorption of food so that damage to it is liable to result in a significant developmental delay in childhood. This might be manifested, for example, in insufficient absorption of proteins and the development of edema, or some patients may suffer from severe diarrhea or a vitamin deficiency as a result of insufficient absorption. The thick secretions in the digestive system can also cause intestinal obstruction at an early age as well as liver disease, because of impaired bile secretion. Over 90% of males and 20% of females also suffer from infertility.

The disease can only be diagnosed by genetic testing, but in most cases testing the composition of sweat is sufficient. The diagnosis is established with certainty if the sweat has an above normal amount of chlorine.

Treatment

The most important treatment is treatment of the lungs. It is important that patients receive regular intensive physical therapy to help them secrete the thick mucus. Lung infection must be treated intensively with antibiotics and some of patients require extended antibiotic treatment, or even continuous preventive therapy. Other drugs are helpful in reducing the viscosity of the mucus and thereby facilitating its removal.

Despite these treatments, some patients reach a stage of progressive pulmonary insufficiency with a process of constant deterioration. At a certain stage the patients find it difficult to carry out simple daily activities and require continuous or intermittent oxygen therapy. Ever since the inception of lung transplants, life expectancy has increased significantly. Patients whose fate was previously sealed are still alive and feel well. Treatment of pancreatic problems is easier and enzyme supplementation can help patients to break down and absorb food. Similarly, it is now easy to replace substances such as vitamins and others that have not been properly absorbed.

Treatment of Cystic Fibrosis at the Dead Sea

Physical activity and respiration therapy improve lung function in cystic fibrosis patients, especially when these activities are performed in groups, as at summer camps and vacation resorts. For several years now Israeli children with cystic fibrosis have spent four weeks each year at summer camps for cystic fibrosis patients in Davos, Switzerland. Davos is situated 1,560 meters (5,118 feet) above sea level so that the amount of oxygen in the air there is far lower than it is at the Dead Sea. Despite the disadvantages of Davos in comparison with the Dead Sea region, after a four-week stay in Davos the children show significant improvement in physical capacity and their ability to undertake difficult physical activities that they were unable to do previously. The good nutrition that they receive and the subsequent weight gain are also of great importance. However, as expected, the stay at Davos does not improve lung function, oxygen saturation or FEV-1.

In 1997, it was reported for the first time that a three-week stay at the Dead Sea brought about significant improvement not only in symptoms but also in lung function. A significant improvement was observed in the FVC and FEV-1 indices and in blood oxygen saturation. Since the participants in the study were children from European countries, there was no follow-up after they returned to their homes and there was no way of knowing how long the improvement lasted.

In 2002, investigators from Soroka University Medical Center published the results of a study they conducted with the participation of 94 Israeli children. The children stayed in the Dead Sea region for a period of three weeks. The objective of the study was to examine not only the influence of their stay at the Dead Sea but also the length of time the benefit lasted after the children returned home. The patients were examined for several days before they went to the Dead Sea (up to a week), three weeks later (just before they left the region) and two months after the end of the treatment. The important results of this study showed a significant improvement of 8.2% in FEV-1 in a comparison between the value measured before they came to the Dead Sea and that measured three weeks later, and an improvement of 7.5%, which lasted for two months after they left the region. Significant improvement was also observed in the blood oxygen saturation, which increased by 1.8% by the end of the treatment period and by 1.3% two months after the end of the treatment. No less important was the significant rise in the patients' weight, which continued for as long as three months.

A recently published study conducted by a group of investigators at the Wingate Institute in Israel examined the effect of a stay at the Dead Sea on several physiological pulmonary indices and the physical ability of 14 cystic fibrosis patients, whose disease severity was classified as medium to severe. The patients were examined before they went to the Dead Sea, once again at sea level, and finally, 72 hours after they arrived at the Dead Sea. The study did not show significant differences in lung function at rest. Nevertheless, oxygen consumption improved significantly at the Dead Sea and an improvement in the lung's ventilatory capacity was observed. A significant improvement was also observed in the blood oxygen level, which enabled patients to carry out more difficult physical activities with greater ease. The investigators emphasized that in addition to the well-known fact that partial oxygen pressure increases with the descent below sea level, air density increases as well. Increased air density also helps to improve physiological pulmonary indices.

In 1984, investigators from Jordan published the results of a study in which they compared the lung function of children living in the Dead Sea region with that of children in the same age group living in Amman, situated at 774 meters (2,539 feet) above sea level. This study did not examine the blood oxygen level of the patients or their physical fitness, but only values of lung volume at rest. No significant difference was observed in any of the values measured between the two groups, a somewhat surprising result; but as mentioned, blood oxygen saturation levels and the ability to undertake physical activity were not measured or compared.

c) Asthma

Controlled experiments have not as yet been conducted on the efficacy of staying in the region for asthma patients. However, a great deal of information has accumulated relating to the improvement seen in most patients, so that I will devote some space to this subject as well.

Asthma is defined as a chronic inflammatory disease of the airways which over-respond to different stimuli. This exaggerated response to stimuli is manifested by constriction of the airways that disappears entirely within a few hours, either spontaneously or as a result of drug therapy. The characteristic symptoms of an asthma attack are shortness of breath, coughing and wheezing. Patients are healthy between attacks.

Asthma is one of the most common chronic inflammatory diseases and its prevalence is increasing in many countries, including the most developed ones. Its prevalence in the United States is, for example, 4-5%. The disease can appear at any age, but in approximately 50% of asthma patients it appears in childhood (up to the age of 19) and in the vast majority of cases it appears by the age of 40. Many factors, both genetic and environmental, can cause the disease or make it worse. The most important genetic factor is atopi, a factor discussed in the section on atopic dermatitis. Here, too, we have an "allergic" cause, so that we sometimes find high levels of the protein IgE, which is characteristic of diseases with an allergic background, in the blood of the sick children. Various external factors can also cause an asthma attack, the most prominent being:

1. Allergens – materials that include certain air-borne antigens (allergens). When these allergens infiltrate the lungs they cause an asthma attack by an immunologic mechanism. For example, pollen from flowers or plants cause asthma when in bloom.

2. Various drugs – such as aspirin, drugs used in the treatment of high blood pressure, and many others.

3. Air pollution – caused by materials emitted into the air by industrial plants, including smoke and others.

4. Occupational causes – exposure to various materials in the work place such as dust, various gases, etc.

5. Infections – this is one of the common causes of exacerbation of asthma. Most infections are viral and do not necessitate treatment with antibiotics.

6. Strenuous physical activity – in some cases an attack occurs during strenuous physical activity.

7. Emotional factors – it is well known that tension and stress can also bring on an attack or make it worse.

As in COPD, the severity of asthma is determined by FEV-1 values. However, while this indicator gets worse in COPD patients as the years pass, in asthma patients it usually returns to normal when the attack is over.

Asthma is defined as mild when the value of FEV-1 is greater than 80% of the normal value; moderate when it is between 60% and 80%; and severe when it is less than 60%.

Therapy

Drug therapy is based on the administration of medication that dilates the airways thereby reducing obstruction and improving symptoms. Some drugs have an immediate effect so they are used during an acute attack, while others have a longer onset of actions so they are used to prevent attacks. The drugs can be injected into a vein or muscle, taken orally, or inhaled through various kinds of inhalers. Steroids are included in the group of drugs whose effect is not immediate and they are given by any of the methods mentioned above, including inhalers. Patients can also be treated with drugs that soften secretions and assist in the removal of mucus. When infection is suspected as the cause of the attack or its exacerbation, treatment with antibiotics should be considered.

Treatment of Asthma at the Dead Sea

As stated above, controlled studies proving the efficacy of a stay in the Dead Sea region have not yet been published. The only study available, published in 1998, was based on the experience accumulated in one of the largest and most important of the clinics in the Dead Sea region, the DMZ Medical Center – Deutsches Medizin Zentrum.

According to the cumulative experience of the DMZ, a stay of four weeks resulted in an improvement in lung function and a reduction in the number of attacks, which were also of diminished severity. The efficacy of the bronchodilators was greater when given to patients staying at the Dead Sea. The authors of the study suggest that magnesium, found in large quantities in Dead

Sea water and in the air, which is absorbed by the skin and the airways, is the cause of the beneficial effect. This hypothesis has not yet been proven scientifically.

d) Sarcoidosis

Sarcoidosis is a disease characterized by the development of tiny structures called granulomas, which can be seen only with a microscope. Granulomas can appear in various body tissues, causing functional impairment. The systems most commonly affected are the lungs, the skin and the eyes. Other systems also may be affected such as the joints, the digestive system, and others. The disease is rare, with a incidence of 10-20 cases per 100,000 population. It generally appears in young adults. The most common symptoms are pulmonary symptoms such as coughing, shortness of breath and chest pains. Other, less common, symptoms are fatigue, weakness, fever and weight loss. On occasion there are no symptoms in which case the disease is diagnosed by an incidental finding in a chest x-ray. The disease can also cause skin rash, inflammation of the internal parts of the eyes (uveitis), and even arthritis. It sometimes affects the heart's conduction system and the coronary arteries and may cause irregularities in the heart rhythm. In rare cases, the central nervous system and the reproductive systems may be affected. The diagnosis is based on chest x-rays in cases of lung involvement, which, as mentioned above, is the most common form, or on a biopsy that shows the characteristic granulomas. In mild cases drug therapy is not always required. In severe cases, especially when the lungs are affected, it is necessary to use steroid drugs over a long period of time. Patients can be cured, but in many cases it recurs, even after a long period of remission.

Since the disease is very rare, only a few cases are known of patients who received treatment at the Dead Sea. All of these patients arrived in the area on their own initiative after despairing of the results from the treatment they received. A Norwegian patient who suffered a severe form of the disease, especially because of lung damage, was completely cured and even stopped taking steroids. The remission lasted for about four months after which the disease returned. The patient came back to the Dead Sea for treatment and after a stay of three weeks all of the symptoms once again disappeared. In other cases as well, significant improvement was observed during the time patients stayed in the region, but to our regret we have no follow-up information on these patients, who were all tourists. It is important to know that in cases of sarcoidosis the joints are sometimes involved and in these cases we can expect improvement in the arthritis. Patients with eye involvement (uveitis) react well to the Dead Sea climate, as will be discussed in the chapter on eye diseases and, thus, if there is evidence that the eyes are affected, improvement can be expected at the Dead Sea.

CHAPTER 8

Health Resorts for the Treatment of Heart Diseases

Heart disease is the number one cause of death in the Western world. The most common heart diseases are those that affect the blood vessels that pump blood to the heart muscle, called the coronary arteries. This disease is called coronary heart disease or ischemic heart disease and is caused by a significant narrowing in the diameter of the blood vessels, or in their complete obstruction. The main cause of the narrowing or obstruction is the creation of atherosclerotic plaques in the walls of the blood vessels. These atherosclerotic plaques contain various materials such as cholesterol, fats, calcium, etc. When the thin layer coating a coronary blood vessel is injured these plaques are exposed to various substances in the blood and an accelerated process of blood clotting is liable to begin, which covers the atherosclerotic plaque and totally obstructs the vessel that was only partially constricted to that point. When the vessel is completely obstructed, a "heart attack" ensues, which is called myocardial infarction; when the obstruction is only partial and some blood still flows in the constricted blood vessel, the result is ischemia, also called angina. Obviously, angina can develop into myocardial infarction. The atherosclerotic plaques develop in a slow process that goes on for many years, until it results in the well-known clinical symptoms.

We know from post-mortem examinations that atherosclerotic plaques were already present in the coronary arteries of young, otherwise healthy soldiers killed in battle. Many factors accelerate the development of the atherosclerotic plaques, some hereditary and others acquired. These are called "risk factors." A brief summary of these risk factors follows.

Genetic Risk Factors

We know of several important genetic risk factors that can cause this condition to develop, or can accelerate its progress, such as disturbances in blood fats, diabetes and hypertension. The incidence of coronary artery disease increases dramatically after menopause, apparently the consequence of a deficiency in the female hormone estrogen although, paradoxically, alternative treatment with this hormone is liable to result in the appearance of this disease or its increased severity. The disease is also more common in some families.

Acquired Risk Factors

The main acquired risk factors are smoking, obesity, thyroid disease, anemia, chronic lung disease, lack of regular physical exercise, and acute or chronic stress. Smoking is one of the most important factors, especially when the heart attack occurs at a young age.

It is important to know that heart disease can appear without any preliminary symptoms and may even result in sudden death at a young age, so that it is often compared with an iceberg, whose visible part is miniscule compared to the part that cannot be seen.

We will not expand our description of the diagnosis and treatment of coronary heart disease, but we will stress the importance of physical activity as preventive therapy, or of rehabilitation therapy following a heart attack or after bypass surgery, since in this respect the Dead Sea has advantages over any other site on earth.

Many studies have shown that carefully supervised physical activity reduces the incidence of death in patients who have recovered from heart attacks or bypass surgery. Physical activity also improves the fitness of patients who suffer from coronary artery disease but have not had a heart attack, and contributes to a decline in death rates. Physical activity following myocardial infarction used to be limited to patients up to the age of 65, but today physical activity as part of the rehabilitation program is not restricted by age. Despite its great importance, only 10% of patients get the opportunity to engage in physical activity as part of their rehabilitation following myocardial infarction. Women are mostly ignored, in comparison with men, and the percentage of women who take part in a heart rehabilitation program is much lower than men. Aside from reducing mortality rates from heart attacks, rehabilitation through physical activity has other advantages: improved function of the blood coagulation system, improved fitness that enables patients to participate in more physical activity, improved activity of the joints and muscle, improved balance, and an increase in bone density that reduces the risk of osteoporosis (the loss of calcium from the bones that increases the risk of broken bones). The patients' self-esteem also improves, leading to increased self-confidence, the feeling that they are still worth something and can continue to make a contribution to the welfare of their families and the community. Physical activity also improves sleep quality.

Coronary Artery Disease

It is well known that going to higher altitudes above sea level can worsen the condition of patients suffering from coronary heart disease or heart failure. The reason for the deterioration is lowered oxygen pressure due to its relative dilution, in comparison with that at sea level, which is caused by a drop in barometric pressure. Until not very long ago the prevailing belief, which turned out to be incorrect, was that patients suffering from heart disease should not be allowed to stay at the Dead Sea for fear that this would make their disease worse. As a result, doctors did not allow many heart patients, who also suffered from skin diseases and arthritis, to go for treatment for the latter diseases in the Dead Sea region. In light of what is known about the relationship between barometric pressure and the partial oxygen pressure, as explained in greater detail previously in the chapter on the climatic conditions at the Dead Sea, it is reasonable to assume that the unique climate at the Dead Sea would have a beneficial effect on heart patients.

In 1998, investigators from Bnei Zion Hospital in Haifa, Israel, headed by Prof. Avineder, proved that not only did the condition of heart patients not deteriorate in the Dead Sea region but, quite to the contrary, it improved. Twelve heart patients and six healthy volunteers, all adults, participated in the study. All of the patients and the volunteers took an exercise stress test and a stress echocardiogram (an ultrasound examination of the heart). The patients were examined in Haifa, the place where both they and the volunteers lived, which is situated at an altitude of 130 meters (426 feet) above sea level, and at the Dead Sea, approximately 400 meters (1,312 feet) below sea level. Each test was repeated three times at the Dead Sea: on the day of the patients' arrival and on the third day and fifth days following that. All of the patients had previously participated for more than a year in a heart rehabilitation program that included supervised, controlled physical activity. Some of them had undergone a myocardial infarction and others suffered from stable angina pectoris. None of the patients or volunteers had lung or joint disease.

The major results of this study were:

▶ A 15% improvement (in patients and volunteers) in the amount of time they could continue strenuous physical activity without physical complaints or changes in their electrocardiograms (an electric recording of heart activity), which was recorded during physical effort (on an exercise bicycle).

▶ A significant improvement among the patients in left ventricular contractility during activity and at rest. As expected, no significant change was found among the healthy volunteers in contractility, which was normal prior to the study.

▶ A mild decrease in systolic blood pressure that began on the second day of their stay in the region and was observed in most of the patients and the healthy volunteers.

▶ A slight decrease in heart rate in both the patients and the healthy volunteers.

In summary, this was the first study to show that not only did the condition of patients suffering from coronary heart disease not deteriorate, but it even improved during their stay in the Dead Sea region.

Some patients suffering from coronary heart disease, especially those who had a previous heart attack develop, over the course of years, congestive heart failure. The heart, in its function, is similar to a pump – by orderly contraction it pumps blood to all body parts and tissues. In cases of congestive heart failure the heart is unable to pump a sufficient amount of blood, so that blood accumulates in the tissues, causing many symptoms and significantly reducing life expectancy. Heart failure can also be caused by other diseases, including diseases of the heart valves, primary heart diseases such as cardiomyopathy, hypertension, etc. The main symptoms of congestive heart failure are shortness of breath upon effort, and in severe cases at rest as well, inability of the patient to lie prone, and swelling in the lower limbs, and in severe cases in the belly as well, as a result of the accumulation of fluids outside of the blood vessels. Another reason that congestive heart failure can get worse is that the amount of blood reaching the kidneys is small so that they cannot excrete excess water and sodium. A distinction is made between the two main types of congestive heart failure, left-sided and right-sided. The main symptom of right-sided heart failure is edema (swelling) resulting from fluid that accumulates in the lower limbs, the belly and other places. In left-sided heart failure the fluids accumulate primarily in the lungs and the main complaint is shortness of breath, which may be extremely severe. When congestive heart failure occurs suddenly, a clinical condition called pulmonary edema may ensue, which if not treated immediately could threaten the patient's life. Heart failure is divided into four degrees of severity:

▶ First degree – the symptoms appear only during significant physical effort.

▶ Second degree – the symptoms appear during usual physical activity.

▶ Third degree – the symptoms appear during physical activity that is less strenuous than usual.

▶ Fourth degree – the symptoms occur during rest, without any effort.

This same group of investigators from Haifa conducted another study in which they assessed the effectiveness of climate therapy at the Dead Sea in patients with congestive heart failure that developed as a complication of myocardial infarction. Twelve patients participated in this study, six with second degree and six with third degree congestive heart failure. Four healthy volunteers served as a control group. As in the previous study, these patients were all examined in Haifa prior to going to the Dead Sea and after three days in the region. The test included physical fitness, which was measured as the maximum distance that they could cover in a brisk walk of six minutes, and an echocardiogram to assess the contractility function of the heart muscle and to quantify the cardiac output (the amount of blood the heart pumps in each beat). Each participant also underwent an exercise stress test on a treadmill during which various physiological parameters were checked including blood oxygen saturation prior to and during exercise, oxygen consumption, etc.

The results of the study were very encouraging. The patients were able to cover a greater distance on the treadmill, their blood oxygen saturation increased by 3%, their systolic blood pressure dropped significantly, their cardiac output increased by the impressive amount of 300 milliliters per minute, and their oxygen consumption improved as well. It is noteworthy that significant improvement was also found in patients with the more severe congestive heart failure (3rd degree), and that the healthy controls also showed a similar improvement.

It should be emphasized that the improvement seen in this study was achieved due to the region's unique climatic conditions only. In the chapter that discussed physiological changes that take place while bathing in mineral water I noted that bathing in mineral water per se leads to a notable improvement in cardiac output because it causes a notable increase in the amount of blood that returns to the heart. It is reasonable to assume that if the patients that participated in this study had also bathed in Dead Sea water or in hot springs water the observed improvement would have been even greater. Further studies are required to confirm this assumption.

It is noteworthy that Japanese investigators found that using a dry sauna at 60°C daily for two weeks is just as effective as rehabilitation therapy based on physical activity. This treatment reduced the symptoms of congestive heart failure and improved blood flow in the coronary arteries.

CHAPTER 9

Health Resorts for the Treatment of Intestinal Diseases

Inflammatory bowel disease

The two most common and well-known bowel disorders are Crohn's disease and ulcerative colitis. To date, the only data that we have is limited data on the effect of the Dead Sea on Crohn's disease, so we will only discuss this disease in some detail.

Crohn's disease is characterized by an inflammatory process that involves the intestinal wall and can cause narrowing of the intestine or even its obstruction, complications that are not usually seen in ulcerative colitis. Other potential complications are intestinal perforation (a hole in the intestinal wall) or the development of fistulas, which are channels that develops between loops of intestine interfering with its normal function, or between the intestine and other abdominal organs, or even sinus tracts that connect between the intestine and the skin of the abdominal wall. These fistulas, which usually appear in the anal region, cause considerable pain and suffering and are very refractory to conservative therapy. Crohn's disease can affect the entire gastrointestinal tract or be isolated to specific regions. The area that is most commonly involved is the small bowel (80%), in particular its final section, the terminal ileum. In 50% of the cases both the small and large bowel are involved. In 20% of the cases only the large bowel is involved, in which case the clinical picture is similar to that of ulcerative colitis.

Symptoms

The symptoms of Crohn's disease are varied. The most salient symptoms include fatigue, prolonged diarrhea, abdominal pain, weight loss, fever and gastrointestinal tract bleeding. Typically the disease begins at a young age with most of the cases developing up to age 35, although it can appear in much older individuals as well. In about a third of the cases there are external signs of disease such as purulent sores or pus-secreting fistulas in the anal and rectal areas, which in some case may be the presenting symptom. Crohn's disease is considered a systemic illness, in other words it can involve other systems in addition to the gastrointestinal system. Skin involvement in the form of purulent sores is quite common and some of the patients develop a type of arthritis that is similar to ankylosing spondylitis. The disease can also involve the eyes causing inflammation of the uvea (uveitis), the inner part of the eye.

The disease is fairly easy to diagnose on the basis of the symptoms and tests, such as colonoscopy (introduction of a flexible tube containing fiber optics through the anal canal). This enables good visualization of the colon in its entirety as well as the taking of biopsies to confirm the diagnosis. Other imaging techniques can also be used such as computerized tomography (CT).

The disease is chronic. In some cases the patients may enter prolonged clinical remission. There is no consensus as to whether the disease reduces life expectancy. In many cases surgery is required to overcome the various complications.

Treatment of Crohn's Disease at the Dead Sea

In 1989 a report appeared in the literature showing that hyperbaric therapy can help heal perianal fistulas in Crohn's patients. In this treatment patients are placed in a pressure chamber in which the atmospheric pressure can be raised artificially way beyond normal pressure (as measured at sea level). The pressure used by the investigators was 2.4 atmospheres, which is much higher than the pressure at the Dead Sea. Clearly, the amount of time that can be spent in this chamber is limited for fear of various complications. In contrast one can stay at the Dead Sea without time limit since the atmospheric pressure is only slightly higher than normal. Hyperbaric therapy has been shown to be effective in the healing of sores and ulcers that are common in patients with diabetes mellitus. In some hospitals, for example in Russia, there are special departments of hyperbaric therapy for a broad range of diseases (not only deep diving accidents) and there are different types and sizes of pressure chambers in which patients can be placed and treated simultaneously.

In 1995 investigators from Israel reported that six patients with severe, active Crohn's disease, which did not respond to standard therapy (including four patients with purulent perianal fistulas), improved significantly after spending one to three week at the Dead Sea. Naturally these patients did not bathe in the Dead Sea because of the severe pain that the fistulas would have caused upon contact with the salt water. The index used by the investigators to assess disease activity and severity decreased from 9.0 to 3.5 after one week and to 2.0 after three weeks at the Dead Sea (the higher the value the more active and severe the disease). In one patient the fistula closed and healed after two weeks and in two other patients there was considerable improvement in the fistulas. In two patients, whose disease was particularly severe and who required treatment with cortisone, the improvement was significant and enabled discontinuation of this medication. In general, the improvement in disease activity occurred before the improvement in the fistulas.

Of course, the number of patients in this study was too small to reach a definitive conclusion as to the effectiveness of the Dead Sea in this disease.

CHAPTER 10

The Dead Sea and Eye Diseases

Uveitis

The uvea is the middle part of the eye and includes the iris, the ciliary body and the choroid. Uveitis is usually accompanied by pain and in severe cases can severely impair vision, even causing blindness. The symptoms that characterize the disease are varied and include redness of the eye, pain and visual impairment. There are cases in which pain is absent and visual impairment is the only symptom. The disease tends to have recurrent flare-ups and the patient is entirely healthy in between. The diagnosis can be reached without difficulty by any trained ophthalmologist. The disease usually involves only one eye.

Uveitis can be an independent entity (primary disease) or can appear in association with systemic diseases – diseases that involve many body systems including the eyes. Among the systemic diseases in which uveitis can appear it is particularly important to note different types of inflammatory joint diseases such as ankylosing spondylitis, psoriasis-associated arthritis, systemic lupus erythematosus, vascular inflammatory diseases, Behcet's disease, juvenile arthritis, inflammatory bowel disease such as ulcerative colitis and Crohn's disease, kidney diseases, trauma to the eye, etc. Various bacteria and viruses can also cause uveitis. The treatment of uveitis is based primarily on steroids administered directly into the eye or systemically. In severe cases various cytotoxic drugs are added to the regimen. These are poisonous drugs that can destroy growth cells by infiltrating them.

Treatment of Uveitis at the Dead Sea

At the end of the 1980s and the beginning of the 1990s evidence began to accumulate that patients with uveitis improve after spending time at the Dead Sea. The first study, which was conducted in 1988 by Dr. Manthey from Germany, showed that in 39% of 45 patients who spent three weeks in the region there was evidence of improvement three months later, including a significant improvement in visual acuity and in near vision. In addition there was a significant reduction in the number of disease flare-ups.

The most comprehensive study, which was published in 2005, was conducted by the ophthalmologist Dr. Ronit Yagev from the Soroka University Hospital in Israel. The study was based on 55 patients, mostly tourists from abroad, who suffered from chronic uveitis and stayed at the Dead Sea for three to four weeks. All the patients were examined immediately upon arrival at the Dead Sea and several other times in the course of their stay there. A significant improvement was achieved in all study measures, including near and distant visual acuity and microscopic findings typical of disease flare-ups. Sixty-four percent of the patients reported that they needed less medication following their stay at the Dead Sea, and that there was a reduction in the number and severity of their attacks. Since the patients were all from abroad it was impossible to conduct a regular follow-up to determine how many months the improvement lasted. Unfortunately, no information was provided as to other diseases that the patients had such as various inflammatory joint diseases or inflammatory bowel disease that could also have caused uveitis. The study did not provide details as to whether the improvement was greater in cases of uveitis secondary to other diseases or in primary cases. The investigators assume that the ultraviolet B radiation that affects the immune system was the major reason for the improvement.

CHAPTER 11

The Dead Sea and Diseases of the Nose

Allergic Rhinitis

The primary characteristics of allergic rhinitis are short periods (day to weeks) of sneezing, runny nose, nasal congestion, and a feeling of itching in the eyes, nose and palate that appear, for the most part, in certain seasons of the year as a result of the infiltration of substances termed "allergens" into the respiratory system. These allergens affect the immune system, which produces antibodies against them. The antibodies cause damage to the nasal mucosa and the upper respiratory tract. The disease is very common with a prevalence of 10-40% in the adult population. It is very rare in children under the age of five and reaches its peak at school age and adolescence. It rarely starts in people older than 50. The disease is very common in industrial areas and in cities and is more common in males. It is more common in families in which other members have suffered from obstruction of the sinus passages, so some of the patients also suffer from higher rates of bacterial sinusitis necessitating antibiotics. Treatment is based, among other things, on nose drops to reduce congestion and relieve symptoms. Nose drops, which can also be administered as a spray, sometimes contain steroids whose function is to reduce the immunological process. Some drops do not contain steroids but rather salt solutions. These are meant to reduce the edema by absorbing fluids from the congested nasal mucosa.

Two interesting recently-published studies conducted in the United States compared the effectiveness of nose drops that contain Dead Sea salts in high concentrations, giving them greater fluid absorptive capacity than drops that contain regular salt (NaCl) solutions or drops that contain steroids. The drops that contain Dead Sea salts were more effective in reducing congestion and reducing symptoms.

In another study on 15 patients, conducted in 2005 by Dr. Cordray et al. from the United States, the investigators compared the effectiveness of Dead Sea nose drops that were given to patients for a week in the form of a spray to steroid nose drops that were also given as a spray. On the basis of questionnaires that the patients answered and an examination by a certified specialist the investigators found a significant improvement with both types of spray, but the steroid containing drops were somewhat more effective. However, it is important to emphasize that prolonged treatment with a steroid-containing spray can cause unpleasant adverse effects that do not occur with a Dead Sea salt containing nasal spray.

Another study, with 42 participants, conducted by Dr. Friedman from the United States in 2006, compared the effectiveness of a spray containing Dead Sea salts with a spray that contained regular salt (NaCl). The spray with Dead Sea salts was more effective, as reported from questionnaires answered by the patients and by a nasal examination by a specialist.

In summary, patients with isolated allergic rhinitis can rely on a nasal spray that contains Dead Sea salts to alleviate their condition and do not need to come to the Dead Sea area for this purpose.

There is no information about other allergic conditions that are relieved by staying at the Dead Sea. In theory there could be an improvement in the condition of patients who suffer from diseases caused or exacerbated by allergens inhaled into the upper respiratory tract, since there is a scarcity in the region of industrial plants that pollute the air and vegetation that can also serve as a source of allergens (for example, pollen that is carried in the wind).

CHAPTER 12

Contraindications and Adverse Effects of Treatment at the Dead Sea

One of the advantages of treatment at health spas is the paucity of serious adverse effects that could threaten the life of the patient or cause severe, permanent damage. However, it is important to know that no medical treatment is entirely devoid of adverse effects. Even when double-blind, controlled trials are conducted to assess the adverse effects of a certain drug compared to a placebo, 5-10% of the adverse effects are seen among the patients who receive the placebo.

The adverse effects of Dead Sea therapy can be classified into two types: serious adverse effects that are liable to threaten life and mild adverse effects that do not cause permanent injury.

Potentially Life-threatening Adverse Effects

"Near Drowning"

Because of the high concentration of salts in Dead Sea water and the floating effect it is impossible to drown in it. However, cases that are known as "near drowning" in the Dead Sea can be dangerous and necessitate immediate treatment to prevent late complications and possible death.

The amount of dissolved salts in Dead Sea water is about 10-fold that of the water in the Mediterranean Sea. The concentration of salts are also much higher, for example the concentration of chorine ions is 10 fold, magnesium ions – 30 fold, sodium ions – 2.8 fold, calcium ions – 36 fold, potassium ions – 16 fold, and bromine ions – 70 fold. The clinical symptoms and the laboratory findings in "near drowning" depend primarily on the amount of water taken into the digestive tract by swallowing or into the lungs by aspiration. In most cases the reason for "near drowning" is a sudden loss of balance. The individual falls into the water and swallows or aspirates even a small amount of water. The aspiration of water into the lungs usually causes initial pulmonary symptoms while swallowing water leads to a dangerous increase in the patient's blood calcium and magnesium levels.

Respiratory Disturbances

Studies conducted on dogs showed that significant clinical symptoms already appear ten minutes after infusion of a small amount of Dead Sea water into the trachea. The dogs developed dyspnea with a significant decrease in blood oxygen saturation that quickly deteriorated to a serious condition termed "chemical pulmonary edema." This edema is characterized by damage to pulmonary blood vessel walls that leads to a transition of fluids into the lung spaces. In most cases the dogs had to be ventilated mechanically until the serious condition passed in order to save their lives.

Electrolyte Disturbances

Swallowing of Dead Sea water often causes a significant increase in the blood concentration of several ions, which could threaten the patient's life. The gravity of the problem and time to its appearance depend on the amount of swallowed water. The two main electrolyte disturbances are increased blood calcium and magnesium concentrations. This phenomenon occurs rather quickly, in less than an hour, and reaches its peak in a few hours. The increase in calcium levels causes a state of disorientation, muscle weakness, and even loss of consciousness. High calcium concentrations can also cause dangerous disturbances in the heart rate and in the conduction of its electrical stimulus. The increase in magnesium concentration mainly causes damage to the nervous and muscular systems, which is manifested as severe muscle weakness to the point of paralysis of the respiratory muscles. The increase in the calcium concentration, like the increase in the magnesium concentration, has a characteristic expression in the electrocardiogram (the recording of the heart's electrical activity).

In order to prevent the development of these serious complications a trained team has to provide immediate initial treatment in the region itself, without waiting for the patient to reach the hospital. The earlier the therapy is started, the better the patient's condition and the better their chance to recuperate without permanent damage.

The initial on-site treatment for near drowning includes placement of a nasogastric tube and gastric lavage with the aim of removing the swallowed, but still unabsorbed, fluid from the gastric mucosa. In addition an intravenous line is established and a diuretic is administered intravenously to increase the renal elimination of calcium and magnesium thereby reducing the danger inherent in increased blood levels. The physician providing this care must be trained in all aspects of resuscitation.

Treatment in the hospital is guided by the patient's condition. In severe cases it may be necessary to carry out dialysis for a short period of time in order to accelerate the elimination of calcium and magnesium.

In 1985 investigators from Jerusalem reported that four of eight patients who were treated for cases of "near drowning" died, a mortality rate of 50%. Some died as a result of disturbances in the heart rhythm or from congestive heart failure due to increased blood calcium and magnesium levels and others died of respiratory failure. In 2003 investigators from the Soroka Medical Center summed up their experience in the treatment of 69 patients who were rushed to the hospital with the diagnosis of "near drowning." Most of the patients had elevated blood calcium and magnesium levels, 29 developed respiratory failure and 11 required mechanical ventilation for a short period of time. Sixty-five patients recovered completely and four had minimal residual damage. The most important message was that all the patients recovered without a single case of death. Today the syndrome is better recognized and treatment has improved to the point where therapeutic success is much higher than reported 15 years ago or more.

Mild Adverse Effects

Treatment at the Dead Sea can also have mild adverse effects that usually pass without leaving permanent damage. The main adverse effect, which results from exposure to the sun, is sunburn. In the past this was a common adverse effect because the period of time that patients spent in the sun was too long. Today, in light of knowledge that has accrued, exposure time is much shorter and the rate of sunburn, which in the past reached as much as 8.2%, has decreased considerably.

It is important to emphasize that despite prolonged periods spent in sunlight, in most cases there has been no evidence of an increase in the number of cases of skin cancer such as melanoma, even though one of its major risk factors is exposure to sunlight, or of an increased number of other types of skin cancer. Although most studies found no evidence of increased skin cancer rates after sun exposure, investigators from Scandinavia, who conducted a long-term follow-up of 1,738 patients from Denmark who were treated at the Dead Sea, reported an increase in the incidence of malignant skin lesions in these patients, particularly non-melanoma skin cancer.

Some physicians and investigators believe that prolonged exposure to the sun accelerates skin aging to some degree and causes skin blemishes, which are common among the elderly. There is no consensus on this issue, however.

Bathing in mineral water or in Dead Sea water may also cause other mild skin problems such as rashes and itching, as well as exacerbation of skin rashes that were present before the initiation of therapy.

If the temperature of the water is not above 38°C-39°C there is no danger that the body temperature will rise above normal. Bathing in higher temperatures could be dangerous because it could cause a significant rise in the body's internal temperature.

Reports from different health spas in Europe provide evidence of various infections that have affected bathers in pools. These pools contained mineral water that was contaminated by various types of bacteria that, at times, caused serious illness. Infections of this type cannot occur in the Dead Sea or in its springs because of the high salt content of the water that prevents the growth and proliferation of bacteria. Of course, patients with open sores can suffer from severe pain while bathing.

Wearing mud packs can also cause mild, transient skin problems, such as itching and various rashes. It is important to emphasize that the mud is completely sterilized, so it cannot cause infection. Most clinics use mud only once and do not recycle it. It is very important that the mud be free of any waste products such as small stones. Overheating of mud can cause burns. Mud can be heated to higher temperatures than mineral water – even up to 50°C.

Because of the region's severe heat, especially in the summer months, it is important to drink a large amount of water to prevent dehydration. Dehydration is an even greater danger in adults who suffer from other diseases and who are not used to the unique climatic conditions of the region.

Contraindications to Treatment at the Dead Sea

We will differentiate between absolute and relative contraindications. Absolute contraindications completely prohibit use of a particular therapeutic method because it can cause death or severe adverse effects. In contrast, relative contraindications do not lead to prohibition of the use of a particular therapeutic method, but necessitate rigorous, continuous monitoring because it can cause various adverse effects that do not, however, threaten the life of the patient or cause serious or permanent damage.

Absolute Contraindications

The few absolute contraindications to Dead Sea treatments are derived from the main danger of drowning or "near drowning."

Bathing in Dead Sea or spring water should be prohibited if there is an actual danger that the patient could lose either consciousness or their balance and fall in the water. Thus, patients who suffer from epilepsy or other diseases of the nervous system, serious disturbances of the heart rhythm, severe uncontrolled diabetes mellitus (that is sometimes accompanied by loss of consciousness), and other diseases should not be allowed to bathe alone. In some circumstances they can be allowed to bathe if sometimes is with them at all times.

Treatment in health spas is not recommended for patients who suffer from acute mental health disorders and are not aware of the dangers inherent in the various therapies.

Treatment in the Dead Sea is also prohibited for patients with severe infections and high fever, especially if there is suspicion of sepsis (presence of the infective bacteria in the blood stream).

One should remember that the Dead Sea area is far removed from any medical center that can provide effective therapy in emergencies that require, for example, mechanical ventilation or administration of certain drugs that are only available in intensive care units. It takes an hour for an ambulance to reach either Beer Sheva or Jerusalem. Patients who suffer from other serious diseases and whose condition might deteriorate suddenly must recognize the danger that they are placing themselves in, even if their disease is not considered a contraindication to bathing in the region.

Relative Contraindications

1. Photosensitivity

Several skin diseases, as well as general disorders, are characterized by photosensitivity with skin rashes or itching that appear after exposure to the sun, even for a short period of time. Naturally, these patients have to avoid staying in the sun. If they avoid exposure to the sun they can still receive any hydrotherapy treatment in Dead Sea water or springs on the condition that they are treated in covered pools. It is important to understand that exposure to the sun can cause not only a skin rash but exacerbations or flare-ups of their particular disease, as is seen, for example, in patients with systemic lupus erythematosus (SLE). Many drugs may also cause skin rashes if the patient is exposed to the sun after taking them, so it is always advisable to consult with a physician before coming to the region.

2. Disease of the veins

Most health spas recommend that patients with varicose veins (dilatation of the veins) on their lower legs avoid treatment in mineral water, especially if it's very hot, because of the danger of exacerbating the condition. Very few scientific studies have assessed this issue. It would appear that there is no real reason to keep patients with mild to moderate venous insufficiency from receiving these treatments unless they have ulcers or open sores as a complication of their disease. These treatments are also appropriate for patients with varicose veins without signs of inflammation. Studies in which the investigators assessed various indices of blood flow in patients with varicose or inflamed veins and in healthy controls failed to find any difference in any of these measures after a single stay of at least 60 minutes in heated mineral water (it should be noted that this period of time is three times longer than the usual recommended time). Treatment is prohibited only in cases where there are unhealed ulcers or sores resulting from severe inflammation of the veins.

Diseases that are Neither Absolute
Nor Relative Contraindications

1. Malignancy

In the past, patients with various types of cancer were not allowed to receive treatment at health spas. It was argued that the various treatments, especially those based on spending time in hot water or hot mud, could accelerate cancer spread. This contention is unproven, and today some forms of therapy for patients with different types of cancer are based on heating the cancer site at high temperatures.

2. Hypertension

Only a few studies have documented changes in blood pressure when entering areas below sea level. In one of the studies, published in 1988, investigators from the Soroka University Medical Center showed that not only did blood pressure not rise in patients with or without hypertension, but actually dropped significantly. In this study, a group of 72 patients (24 with hypertension and 48 with normal blood pressure) was studied at the Dead Sea. The investigators found that the systolic blood pressure (the higher value) dropped by an average of 18 mm of mercury (mmHg) and the diastolic blood pressure (the lower value) dropped by an average of 8 mmHg. This improvement in blood pressure continued throughout the patients' stay in the region. When blood pressure was measured when the patients bathed in hot spring water an additional slight drop in the systolic and diastolic blood pressure was measured in patients with normal blood pressure and a slight increase in systolic blood pressure in patients with hypertension. For technical reasons, blood pressure could not be measured in patients while they actually bathed in the Dead Sea, but measurements that were taken immediately after they came out of the water showed a slight increase in the systolic value only in patients with normal blood pressure. This study, like several additional studies, proved that patients with hypertension can stay in the region and receive all treatments without concern.

3. Severe, active inflammatory joint disease

As mentioned above, patients suffering from severe, active inflammatory joint diseases can receive any treatment without concern that their condition will get worse. In spite of this, many doctors, even rheumatologists who are unfamiliar with this issue, recommend, without justification, that their patients not go to the Dead Sea, thus keeping them from getting treatment that could help them and relieve their suffering.

CHAPTER 13

The Contribution of Dead Sea Minerals to Skin Beauty *

by Dr. Ze'ev Ma'or

Dead Sea Cosmetics – From Fairy Tale to the World of Science

Venus (as depicted in Botticelli's famous painting) arose from the sea, perhaps because like the waves of the sea, beauty is also deep, rich and incomprehensible. From time immemorial beauty and the sea have been linked together. That is why people from around the world go to the sea and find in it natural forces of vitality and beauty. Sea mud, salt water alga and plankton play roles as important agents in many beauty preparations. It is no wonder that minerals from our deep and unique salty Dead Sea were linked to beauty sold in jars for cosmetic purposes.

Cleopatra was certainly not the first one who used Dead Sea minerals, but apparently she was the only one who requisitioned all its treasures for herself. To be sure that she had no competition for the rank of the most beautiful woman in the world she paid

* The author is a researcher in the Dead Sea Research Center of the Ministry of Science and Vice President for Research and Development in the Ahava Dead Sea Laboratories (AHAVA)

good money to the Hasmonean kings who sold her these unique treasures containing sea water and mud.

"My lover is for me a cluster of henna from the vineyards of Ein Gedi," writes the author of the Song of Songs and hints at the medicinal and cosmetic herbs of the Dead Sea region. In the ancient synagogue of Ein Gedi there is a mosaic inscription: "Cursed be he who delivers the city's secrets to strangers," and researchers are convinced that this is in reference to the production of persimmon perfume. Archeologists assume that the remains that were uncovered at several sites along the sea coast are witness to the developed cosmetic and perfume industry that has existed in this region for as long as it has been recorded. From here, the lowest point on the earth, caravans departed from early times loaded with landanum, balm, myrrh, frankincense and persimmon headed for the halls of Rome, Greece and Egypt, to the rich markets hungry for unique cosmetics.

With the renewal of settlements in the Dead Sea region people again started to use mineral treatments offered at health spas along its shores – at Neve Zohar, Ein Bokek and Ein Gedi. Later on the first attempts were made to package minerals in bottles as preparations that could be taken home. At first only mud, salts and sea water were packaged and later on real cosmetic preparations were developed. Recognition as a pioneer is reserved, apparently, for Dr. Amira Vida and Lon Cosmetics, Ltd., who, in the 1960s, inaugurated the first production line based on Dead Sea minerals. Like many attempts, this line was also "ahead of its time" and did not survive the test of time.

Today Dead Sea cosmetics flourish, and this historical tale, which is spiced with legends from the days of the Queen of Sheba and Cleopatra, is sold together with the smells and brands of Dead Sea minerals throughout the world. In my estimate there are at least 70 brands of Dead Sea minerals that are sold in Israel and the world. In some of the brands the minerals are put in preparations in miniscule concentrations and serve only as "marketing décor." Based on its composition chemists can easily discern the preparation's stable emulsion and its sensitivity to the presence of salts. If we take a preparation of this type and drip a small amount of Dead Sea saline water, we will immediately see how the emulsion collapses and the cream loses its original texture. Of course, there are also cosmetic lines that are actually based on Dead Sea salts. These were formulated by a large amount of work based on scientific research and they succeed in harnessing the minerals that yield cosmetic preparations that really work on the skin. These lines always have salts, Dead Sea water, spring water and even black mineral mud in active quantities.

But what do the sea water, the black mud and the salt crystals really contain that turns them into a commodity in demand by pharmacies and perfumeries throughout the world? Why do so many women prefer to go to sleep with the saline serum "Osmoter" and to wake up with a black skin mud mask on their faces? I have also tried to solve this Dead Sea enigma and for almost twenty years I have been searching for scientific proof of this magic, which I will try to describe in the next section.

The Elements of the Dead Sea from which the Preparations Are Made

"The answer must be found in nature," wrote Hippocrates the Greek in the 5th century and, indeed, from the earliest times people have sought after active natural elements. Without doubt the Dead Sea and its adjacent desert environment have a unique mixture of active ingredients with healing properties. These substances join together in an historic tale, in a charmed atmosphere, in the tranquility of the region and the magic, almost mystic air that is so suited for cosmetics. We, "the fishermen of the Dead Sea," discover the active Dead Sea elements by conducting geological and hydrological surveys and by producing them at an industry-level quality, and we concoct preparations to nurture the skin. The list of source elements includes, first of all, mineral components: black mud, salty sea water, crystalline bath salts and spring water. Organic elements that are characteristic of the flora and fauna of the Dead Sea region and the Judean desert are added to the list. The most important of these is the unicellular alga Dunaliella salina, which can survive even in the Dead Sea. This alga was discovered in the Dead Sea by Elazar Vulcani in 1940 and is considered an excellent source of beta-carotene (a compound that is transformed into Vitamin A in the body). Today it is grown in salt water pools in the Arava desert and in nylon sleeves at the University of Beer-Sheva. Plants from the Judean desert also contain valuable compounds for the Dead Sea beauty industry, among which *Ziziphus spina-christi* and palm dates are noteworthy. In the past the perfumed plants in the Dead Sea region, the persimmon and the myrrh, were famous throughout the ancient world. We know that these were expensive plants, but their exact identity is not known to modern researchers, and the methods used to produce aromatic perfume from this plant substance has been lost over the years and become an enigma. Among the organic compounds that come from the Dead Sea and were used for skin preparations are bitumen and tar. This is an oil-saturated organic substance which, until about 40 years ago, was released from the sea bottom and floated on its surface. Effective skin preparations have been produced from bitumen. Another ancient Dead Sea substance was the poison that was milked from snakes caught in the past in the Judean desert and along the Dead Sea coast and was used in the ancient pharmaceutical industry. I will focus on the contribution of mineral compounds for cosmetic products.

The various mineral compounds are very different from each other in composition. These are natural mixtures that were produced by nature over the course of hundreds of years. Frequently the chemical constitution provides documentation of the history of these compounds. For example, the black mud that is collected on the northern shore of the Dead Sea tells the story of the Jordan River, and it contains clay that was transported from the distant northern mountains by water from snow that melted on Mount Hermon. In contrast, mud that is mined at the foot of Masada is rich in soil that came in torrents from Judean mountain floods. The thickness of the layer teaches us about the level of precipitation that year. The white stripes in the mud are evidence of dry and moist periods. The composition of spring water reflects the aquifer from which it flowed and is different in sulphur content from one spring to another as determined by the source, located deep in the belly of the earth. The sea water in the deep northern basin is different in composition from the pool waters in the southern Dead Sea, because this water was transported thus skipping the initial precipitation of table salt in the sunlight, along the way. Research and development personnel, who are responsible for the development of Dead Sea products, have to be very familiar with this spectrum of substances that have been discovered from geological and hydrological surveys. They have to characterize each component on the basis of its chemical composition and physical properties. Only then can they compose the right combination of different compounds from the Dead Sea and other sources and prepare a quality cosmetic product based on Dead Sea minerals.

The main mineral elements (in terms of content) in Dead Sea water are magnesium (Mg), calcium (Ca), sodium (Na), and potassium (K). These metals are found in the water as salt solutions. People involved in the development of cosmetic products prefer compounds composed more of magnesium and calcium and less of sodium and potassium, and especially try to avoid high sodium levels since they feel that sodium salts cause an unpleasant itching feeling when they come into contact with the skin. The relative bromine level among the other salts is also important since it is believed to calm the body and the soul. Is it also important that there are no iodine ions in the sea water. Many people in the world who suffer from endocrinological problems are happy to learn that they can use sea products without fear of iodine sensitivity. Many other elements are contained in Dead Sea salts and a few of them, despite their low concentrations, are considered contributors to the Dead Sea mystique. Noteworthy among these are zinc (Zn), iron (Fe), sulphur (S) and strontium (Sr).

The Effect of Dead Sea Minerals on Skin Quality

From early times people have credited Dead Sea minerals with the ability to improve skin appearance in general. In the past, when preparations were formulated, the subjective opinion of various male and female testers was relied upon to assess their value, but today this is not enough and researchers test the effect of minerals on the skin using skin models in the laboratory and clinical trials on the skin of volunteers. Many contend that the minerals add moisture to cells because of their hygroscopic property, which is manifested by their propensity to absorb water. Indeed, within the cells they are an important element in determining the natural moisturizing factor (NMF) of skin cells. Other researchers explain that the minerals, when placed on the skin as cosmetics, turn into an osmotic pump that sucks up the fluids from the inner layers of the dermis and transmits them to the surface of the skin, the epidermis. Thus, improved nutrition of the skin and an increased moisture level are achieved by means of this osmotic pump. For this reason, or for other unknown reasons, Dead Sea minerals are considered a skin moisturizing element, and, indeed, a significant increase in the level of skin moisture was measured by a corneometer after mineral-containing cosmetics were rubbed on the skin. This success was repeated with other tests of many different cosmetic preparations. Thus, in the book of cosmetic compounds (INCI) the elements of the Dead Sea – the water, the mud and the salts – are listed as humectants, in other words, skin moisturizers.

Many people who have bathed in the Dead Sea and experienced the excitement of floating in it have stated, when coming out of the water, that they felt that their skin became smooth "like a baby's skin." This desire for smoothed wrinkle depths is a wish expressed by many women, who are prepared to spend large sums of money for a cosmetic that can impart a young, smooth look to aged skin. Smoothness of skin is measured nowadays by a sophisticated instrument that tests the depth of wrinkles by means of various optic methods at a large number of spots on the skin surface. These measurements are analyzed on a computer to determine the depth of the wrinkles in the epidermis. Indeed, in a double-blind study, in which neither the doctors or the patients knew who was receiving mineral treatment and who was getting an identical treatment but without minerals, as a control group (placebo therapy), the addition of 1% Dead Sea water to the gel yielded an improvement of over 40% in skin smoothness. This astounding finding was reported in the professional literature and patents were registered for the unique mineral components that were found to be particularly effective in smoothing the skin.

Smoothing the skin and adding moisture to the epidermis are, indeed, two welcome actions for which Dead Sea minerals have gained credit as desirable components in many cosmetics. Delaying the aging process is very likely the greatest wish and the most important motive driving the cosmetic market. Many preparations boast of "anti-aging" activity. Of course aging cannot be arrested. The wish of cosmetic manufacturers is more modest than that: to achieve control of the process and to slow down this natural development to the greatest possible extent. Skin aging is caused by a combination of several factors. Among the more important factors are exposure to the sun, particularly ultraviolet radiation (UVA and UVB) and lifestyle (smoking, nutrition, work and rest habits). Genetic factors also play an important role on the rate of aging. At the level of the cell, aging is usually defined as the loss of capacity for cell division and the accumulation of damage to essential cellular elements such as DNA and proteins. In the wake of this damage deleterious metabolic pathways are activated. In the skin laboratory of the Life Sciences Institute of the Hebrew University in Jerusalem, under the supervision of Prof. Yoram Milner, the processes of skin aging have been studied for several years, in collaboration with the research institutes in other universities in Israel and the world.

The Effect of Dead Sea Minerals on Skin Aging at the Biological Level

At the skin laboratory of the Hebrew University the effect of Dead

Sea minerals on skin biology was tested at the cellular level. We used bio-markers manifested by the skin to measure the effect of exposure to mineral mud or Dead Sea water on cells. Since we preferred not to use animal skin we investigated the activity of salts on human skin only. From the results of the tests we conducted we concluded that Dead Sea minerals, when applied to the skin at low concentrations, do have a true biological effect on the skin and do slow down the aging process.

Additional Effects of Minerals on The Skin, as Investigated in Scientific Laboratories

A study of bathing salts from the Dead Sea showed that bathing in a mineral salt solution reduced the expression of inflammatory skin phenomena. These inflammatory skin conditions flare up from time to time, and the cause of the inflammation often cannot be identified. This finding has significance in relation to the role of minerals in skin-care since nowadays there is an increase in immune system activating phenomena and in symptoms of skin inflammation. One study found that mineral mud has significant anti-microbial activity and was especially effective in suppressing the activity of acne-causing bacteria and yeast. This activity is related, apparently, to the release of sulphur compounds from the mud. This finding has great importance for the use of cosmetic mud masks whose effectiveness is recognized for deep cleansing and drying of sores (comedones) on fatty, problematic facial skin.

How Do Minerals Work on the Skin?

There are several possible mechanisms of action of Dead Sea minerals on the skin. In contrast to the explanations that were given in the past, the rubbing of preparations rich in Dead Sea minerals onto the skin does not "nourish the skin with minerals." In a study conducted at the Biological Institute in Nes Ziona we found a very low level of skin permeation by minerals because of the skin's barrier capacity. It is logical to assume that the minerals reach the skin cells primarily by outward diffusion from the internal layers rather than through inward penetration of preparations that are rubbed on the skin. Given that minerals almost do not penetrate skin barrier at all, many investigators have been looking for another satisfactory explanation to solve the enigma of minerals' mechanism of action, since the resulting moisturizing effect, the reduction of wrinkles and the rejuvenation of the skin have been studied and proven valid beyond doubt.

One of the assumptions is that the minerals that are applied to the skin do not "serve" the cells, because of their low permeability, but "teach" the cells how to function correctly, by sending appropriate messages through ion binding.

Although, as stated above, there is still no clear explanation for the way minerals act, the range of results support our assessment that Dead Sea minerals have a great potential effect on the cellular control of central processes including cell division, differentiation, aging and programmed death. The concentration of applied minerals and the way the skin is exposed to them affect the results of their action and stimulate cell division (at low concentrations) or cell cycle arrest (at high concentrations). Therefore, it is important to differentiate between applying preparations on healthy, whole intact skin, which is an effective barrier to mineral permeability, and the application of topical skin preparations to damaged skin, for example in the case of psoriatic lesions. Indeed, studies have shown that Dead Sea salts reduce the rate of psoriatic skin cell division. This fact explains the relief felt in this disease, especially the reduction in the annoying skin plaques, after the sick skin is immersed in mineral preparations.

What Does the Future Hold for the Use of Dead Sea Minerals in the Field of Beauty Nurturing?

It seems to me that we live today in the "mineral age." Minerals have gained a central role not only in food supplements but among the products that await buyers on beauty shelves. The broad range of cosmetics based on minerals today include almost all skin products, and mineral products for hair and nails from wrinkle cream and shampoo to nail hardeners. Name labels that base their marketing efforts on mineral elements can be found in many countries in the world: spring water from France (Vichi, Aven, La-Rosh pose, Biotherm), mud from an Italian health spa (Therma de Saturnia), and salt, mud and our Dead Sea solutions. Cosmetic lines based on Dead Sea labels can be found in pharmacy chains, "mass market" drugstores, and food chains. Dead Sea products are also sold through catalogues, TV shopping channels, and by direct marketing. Youngsters from Israel offer Dead Sea products to customers in stalls set up in shopping malls in London and New York. A "mineral boom" is taking place in the world and this prosperity, the multitude of available products, all of which are sold thanks to their mineral content, can be confusing.

So what does the future hold? Scientific research conducted in laboratories in Israel and throughout the world is elucidating the great contribution of minerals in particular and of Dead Sea preparations in general to skin health. Clinical trials on products containing Dead Sea minerals have proven their anti-aging activity, and their ability to reduce the depth of wrinkles and to add moisture and vitality to skin cells. It is clear to researchers today that mixtures of the unique Dead Sea elements, including, among others, calcium, magnesium, zinc, potassium, bromine and strontium, can help skin affected by various problems and can add beauty, imparting a shinier and more glamorous appearance to healthy skin. Yet, what we do not know still goes way beyond what we do, so it would appear that the enigma of the Dead Sea will continue to be studied for many years to come. The initiation of comprehensive studies using bio- and nano-technology could provide new vigor in coming years and give new life to the minerals that have been harvested for thousands of years from our Dead Sea shores.

CHAPTER 14

Questions and Answers

While giving talks to the general public I have often faced questions that come up repeatedly in different versions. In this chapter I will give my answers to these questions, to focus more on information related to health spas in general and to the Dead Sea in particular.

Question:**Is there a minimum amount of time that one should spend at the Dead Sea?**

In general, the minimum recommended period of time is two weeks for joint diseases and three weeks for skin diseases. Shorter periods of time are less effective and do not produce the most desired result. Also, patients should not return home after each day's treatment, but should stay at the Dead Sea region for the entire treatment period.

Question: **Can pregnant women be treated with mud and can they bathe in Dead Sea water or hot spring water?**

There is no reason not to undergo these treatments during pregnancy. Spring water contains radioactive substances such as radon and radium, but the amount is negligible and there is no risk to either the woman or the fetus.

Question: **Does the therapy have a beneficial effect on male or female fertility?**

There is no proof that therapy is beneficial in problems related to male or female fertility.

Question: **Is it possible to drink the spring water (as is the case in many health spas in Europe) and does this help heal any diseases?**

Drinking spring water is prohibited because of its high concentration of salts and minerals. In Europe there are health spas where different diseases are treated by drinking spring water, but in those cases the water contains elements that are effective in treating some diseases such as recurrent urinary tract infections or kidney stones.

Question: **Which mud is better – hot or cold?**

In many places along the Dead Sea coast bags containing cold mud are sold and the mud is used without heating. There is no doubt that unheated mud is less effective than heated mud. Dead Sea salts can also be bought and dissolved in a heated tub, but this treatment is less effective than actually bathing in Dead Sea water.

Question: **Is the treatment offered at famous health spas in Europe, such as Karlovi-Vari, better and more effective than that offered at the Dead Sea?**

To date no study has been conduced that compared the effectiveness of Dead Sea therapy to that of any European health spa in the same group of patients with the same disease. I have no doubt that the Dead Sea has clear-cut advantages over other health spas, thanks to the unique climatic conditions and the mineral wealth of the Dead Sea and spring water. Many Israeli patients who were treated in both the Dead Sea and in health spas in Europe can bear witness that the Dead Sea is preferable.

Question: **Should one change the dosage of medications or stop taking them at all while undergoing treatment at the Dead Sea?**

In general changing the dosage of specific medications or completely stopping them during the stay at a health spa is not recommended. The primary reason for this is that discontinuation of medications may make it impossible to assess reliably whether the health spa therapy was effective and helped the patient. It is important to remember that sometimes the maximal effect of the treatment appears only at the conclusion of the treatment period or even a while afterwards. However, it is definitely possible to reduce or stop any drugs that do not effect or change disease activity such as analgesics, in accordance with the patient's condition. In many studies investigators even assess the reduction in pain pills as a measure of treatment efficacy.

Question: **Can health spa therapy cure joint or skin diseases?**

The treatment cannot completely cure skin or joint diseases, and is only intended to alleviate the patient's suffering. In many cases complete or partial remission of disease activity can be achieved and usually lasts for several months. Thus, discontinuation of medications is not recommended except in cases of complete and prolonged disease remission.

Question: **Can diseases be prevented by health spa treatments?**

There is no proof that diseases can be prevented by the various treatment administered at health spas. However, one cannot ignore the beneficial effects of these treatments on our physiological system. Just as regular physical activity, for example, can reduce heart disease, it is possible that health spa treatments can help, but this assumption has not been tested to date. Similarly, no epidemiological studies have been conducted to assess whether residents of the Dead Sea region are healthier than similar populations in other areas and suffer less from diseases such as joint or skin disease. It would be interesting to compare, for example, illnesses among members of Kibbutz Ein Gedi to another kibbutz that is not located in the Dead Sea region, but the number of people who live in the Dead Sea region is relatively small and insufficient for epidemiological studies of this type.

Question: **Which season is best for Dead Sea treatments?**

The recommended seasons are spring and autumn, although all types of therapy are available in the summer and winter as well. The summer heat is harsh, especially for patients from other countries, and in the winter the clouds are liable to reduce the efficacy of treatments that are based on the region's unique radiation.

Question: **Is it advantageous to avoid washing the body after bathing in Dead Sea water so as to leave the salt crystals on the skin for an additional period of time and to increase the effect of the therapy?**

There is no reason to remain with salt crystals on the body and a shower is recommended immediately following bathing in the Dead Sea. The optimal time to spend bathing in Dead Sea water is up to two hours per day (one hour in the early morning and one hour in the late afternoon). The amount of time spent bathing in the Dead Sea should be increased gradually.

Question: **Should treatment be prohibited for patients receiving new drugs for joint disease, such as anti-TNF alpha treatment or other new treatments?**

There is no problem in continuing to receive these treatments. However, some drugs are liable to cause adverse effects, especially skin rashes, when the patient is exposed to the sun so it advised to consult with a doctor before coming to the region.

Question: **Can patients with atrial fibrillation or other common heart rhythm disorders receive treatment?**

Definitely yes. Treatment should be avoided only in cases of irregular heart rhythms that cause dizziness or loss of balance and consequently falls or even unconsciousness. In these cases treatment should only be considered if the patient is constantly accompanied by someone who can prevent falling into the water. Patients with implanted pacemakers can also be treated without any problem, but treatment is prohibited for patients with special pacemakers that are also defibrillators (an instrument that works by giving an immediate electric shock in cases of rhythm disturbances that can cause loss of consciousness or endanger patients' lives).

Question: **Can patients who receive anticoagulant drugs be treated?**

This question relates to drugs such as coumadin, sintrom, plavix and aspirin, all of which are taken orally, or heparin and clexan, which are given by injection. These drugs are often used to treat patients with a range of heart diseases or diseases of blood vessels in the brain or extremities. They are also used to prevent complications in patients with diabetes mellitus, hypertension, elevated blood lipids, etc.

Unless they suffer from a disease previously listed as an

absolute or relative contraindication, these patients can definitely receive the various Dead Sea treatments.

Question: **Is it mandatory to undergo a physical examination before beginning treatment?**

Physical examination is not mandatory, but it is recommended for any patient who wants to be more relaxed and feel secure. In addition, patients should get detailed information and explanations on adverse effects, contraindications, and other problems that might occur during treatment.

Question: **Last week I began treatment with mud packs and bathing in the Dead Sea, but I feel worse and more tired. Why?**

The reason for this bad feeling is an adverse reaction called a "thermal reaction." It is caused by changes that take place in the immune system as a result of treatment, and will pass within a few days. There is no need to stop treatment, but it may be helpful to reduce their frequency temporarily until the feeling improves. In general, people who have this reaction actually respond better later on and the final treatment outcome is better than in others who do not have it.

Question: **What is the optimal number of weekly treatments?**

Two treatments per day is the maximum recommended number of treatments (for example, mud and bathing in the Dead Sea). These treatments can be very fatiguing so one day each week should be set aside for rest without any therapy.

Question: **I have a severe joint disease. I spent thee weeks at the Dead Sea and received all treatments, but there was no improvement in my condition. Should I try these treatments again in the future?**

It is most unlikely that there will be improvement in the future, so it would not be logical to come back. Unfortunately, these treatments do not always work, and a relatively small percentage of patients do not benefit from them. It is impossible to tell in advance who will have a positive outcome and who will not.

Question: **My only problem is my knee. Should I rub mud on the painful knee only or on my entire body?**

Treatment with mud packs is considered a systematic therapy, which means that it not only works locally by warming the joint, but also by activating various immunological mechanisms and inhibiting the synthesis of proteins that trigger inflammatory processes. Thus, it is preferable to rub the mud over a large surface and not only on the patient's knee.

Question: **Is there any difference in the effectiveness of treatment when using various Dead Sea spring waters?**

No studies have been conducted to date to compare the effectiveness of treatments from various springs, so the answer to this question is that we do not know at this point.

Question: **Is there a danger of contracting a skin infection after treatment in a sulphur pool?**

The high salt content of the water prevents the growth of most infectious bacteria, so there is no threat whatsoever that a skin infection will develop as a result of the treatment.

Question: **Sometimes I bathe in hot spring waters together with psoriasis patients who shed skin plaques into the water. Can I get psoriasis from this?**

Psoriasis is not an infectious disease, so there is no danger that it can be transmitted by skin plaques that are shed into the water.

Question: **Can patients who suffer from a malignant disease receive these treatments?**

Definitely yes. In the past some people believed that treatments based on warming the body in high temperatures could cause accelerated spread of the tumor. This theory has been disproven. There is no reason not to receive these treatments, especially if there is a good reason for it, including a disease that can be helped by it.

Question: **Are the treatments effective for the treatment of gout?**

No studies have been conducted to date that have proved that treatment at the Dead Sea, especially bathing in Dead Sea water or springs, is effective in this disease, although theoretically it is reasonable to assume that bathing should cause increased excretion of uric acid, as it does in the case of sodium and potassium, thus reducing the frequency and severity of attacks.

Clinics and Health Care Services at Dead Sea Health Spas

Red Magen David Station

The station is located at the solarium in the Ein Bokek hotel area and is manned 24 hours a day. There are two ambulances, one regular and one for intensive care. One additional ambulance is located at Neot Hakikar and another at Kibbutz Ein Gedi.

Emergency clinic

An emergency clinic is located in Ein Bokek and has a staff of on-call doctors. The clinic is active daily from 7 PM to 7 AM the next day. On weekends the clinic is open continually from Friday afternoon at 1 PM until Sunday morning at 7 AM. On holidays and on holiday eves the clinic works on the same schedule as on weekends.

Solarium 400

The solarium, which is located in the heart of the Ein Bokek hotel area, is a large, enclosed sun tanning site that serves patients with skin and joint diseases in particular. It has large suntan yards (separate for men and women), with tanning beds, mattresses, shaded areas, fans, showers, water coolers and wardrobes. It was designed to serve severely handicapped customers. The solarium has an on-site private beach, for men and for women, and many and varied sport facilities. The descent to the water is easy and convenient and is adapted for handicapped customers who need support to enter the water. The place also has an air-conditioned central building, a tourist information station, clinic services, a Red Magen David station and an intensive care ambulance. The solarium is directed by the Tamar local council. The health funds cover the entrance fee to the solarium and members of the Israeli Association of Psoriasis are eligible for a discount.

Telephone: 08-6584484

In the building that houses the solarium clinic there is a separate clinic that provides consultation and treats patients, mostly with skin diseases.

Telephone for the clinic: 08-6520297.

The DMZ Medical Center (Deutsches Medizinisches Zentrum)

This clinic is located in the Lot Spa Hotel and serves tourists and Israelis. It is directed by Dr. Marco Harari, a doctor with broad experience and international recognition in the fields of climate medicine and balneotherapy. Dr. Harari has published numerous papers on clinical trials based primarily on experience that has accumulated in the clinic in the treatment of a broad range of diseases including skin and joint diseases, asthma, etc. Mud treatments are offered at the hotel, which also has covered sulphur pools, sweet water pools, a covered Dead Sea water pool, an exercise room, a sauna, a jacuzzi, massage rooms, etc.

Clinic telephone number: 08-9973117

Health Vacation Center Ltd.

This health vacation center has two branches in the Oasis Hotel (previously the Carlton Hotel). One branch mainly treats various skin diseases and the other, which is also called the Sanus Clinic, treats joint diseases. Treatments include hot mud packs, a sulphur pool, bathing in Dead Sea water, physical therapy and massages. The center employs a permanent general practitioner and various consultants, as required.

MRE European Medical Center

This center was established in 1993 and mainly treats tourists suffering from various joint diseases, skin diseases, eye diseases, and has a general medicine practice. The center's principal doctor is Dr. Hani Giris, a dermatologist, who is in continuous touch with the Dermatology Department of the Soroka University Medical Center in Beer Sheva. The center is located in the Dead Sea Gardens Hotel.
Telephone number: 08-6584338.

The Paula Medical Center

This center is located in the Blue sky Mall and provides conventional and alternative medicine services. The head doctor in the clinic is Dr. Friedman. The clinic provides many treatments including massages, mud, physical therapy, laser therapy, ultrasound, magnetotherapy (treatment by means of magnets), acupuncture, reflexology, exercising, treatment of the lower extremities with oxygen baths, and other modes of alternative medicine.
Telephone: 08-6520001

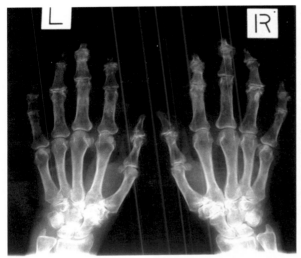

X-rays of the hands of a patient with oteoarthritis.(courtesy of Dr Gideon Flusser)

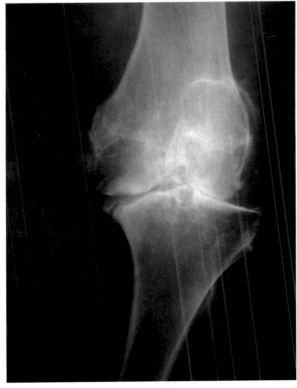

X-rays of the knee of a patient with osteoarthritis. (courtesy of Dr Gideon Flusser)

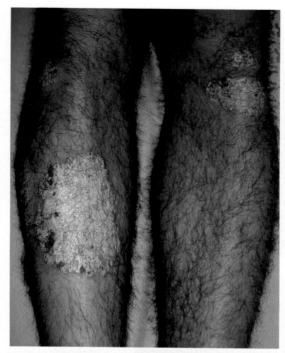

Plaque psoriasis
(courtesy of Dr Dafna
Hallel-Halevy)

Widespread vitiligo
(courtesy of Dr Dafna
Hallel-Halevy)

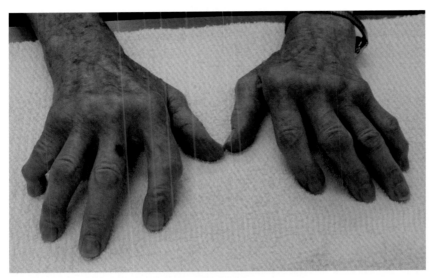

Hands of a patient with psoriatic arthritis

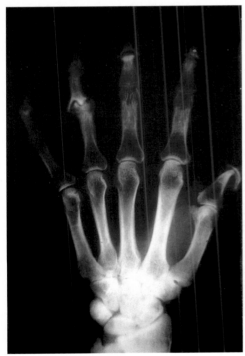

X-rays of hand of a patient with rheumatoid arthritis

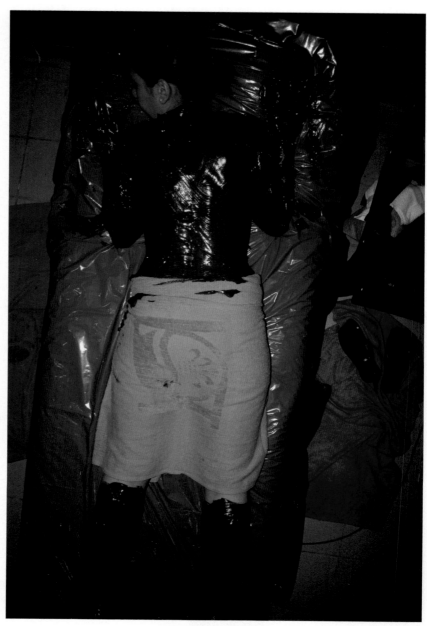

Mud pack therapy

Floating in the Dead Sea

Floating in the Dead Sea covered with a mud pack

Sulfur pool therapy

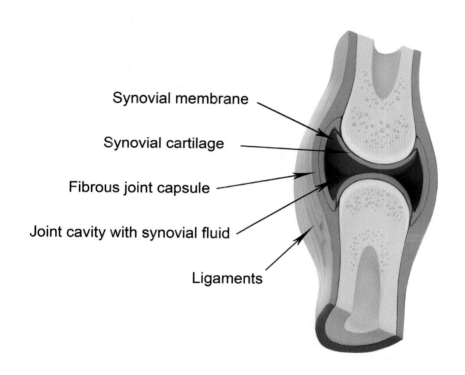

Synovial membrane

Synovial cartilage

Fibrous joint capsule

Joint cavity with synovial fluid

Ligaments

Structure of a synovial joint
(Illustration: Un Atomic Studios)

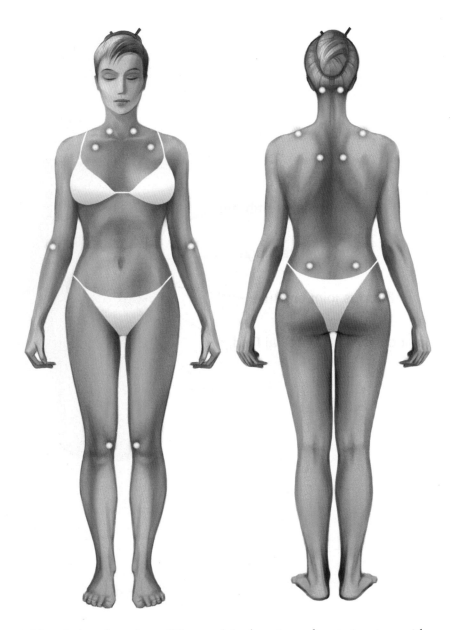

18 typical tender points of fibromyalgia. Anterior and posterior views with identical points on each side of the body
(Illustration: Un Atomic Studios)